ILLUSTRATED HISTORY OF T

MW00717809

BANTAM BOOKS

TORONTO ● NEW YORK ● LONDON ● SYDNEY ● AUCKLAND

STRIKE
AIRCRAFT

by
F. Clifton Berry, Jr.

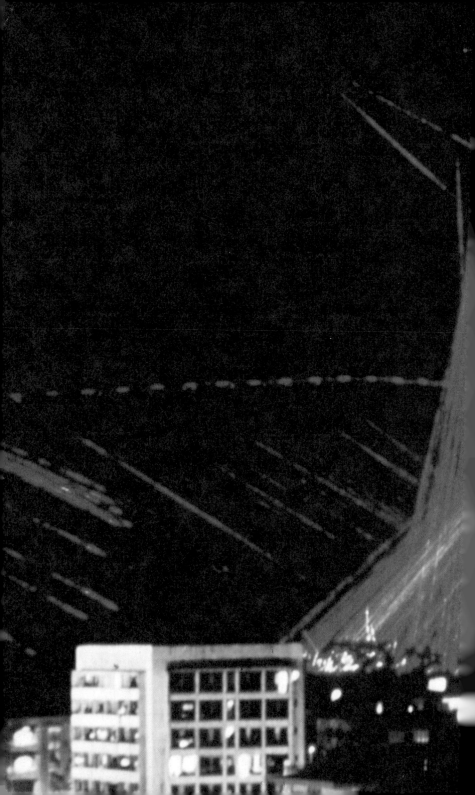

RAIN OF FIRE:

Cannon fire from a gunship lights up the night sky near Saigon. The Lockheed AC-130 Spectre gunship had the most elaborate array of sensors and weapons in Southeast Asia, including electronic devices to detect vehicle engine ignitions, various night vision devices, and on some models an adapted field artillery 105mm howitzer.

BLAST-OFF:

A Republic F-105 Thunderchief on its takeoff roll, afterburners blazing. Big, heavy, and fast, the ''Thud'' flew more than 75 percent of the sorties in the long Rolling Thunder bombing campaign against North Vietnam.

BUFF:

Big Ugly Fat Fella is the polite version of the Boeing B-52's nickname. The world's greatest strategic bomber began its Vietnam combat career playing a lowly ground support role, but moved center stage in the closing days of the war when it was deployed as the firepower arm of a US policy designed to blast the Communists into serious peace talks.

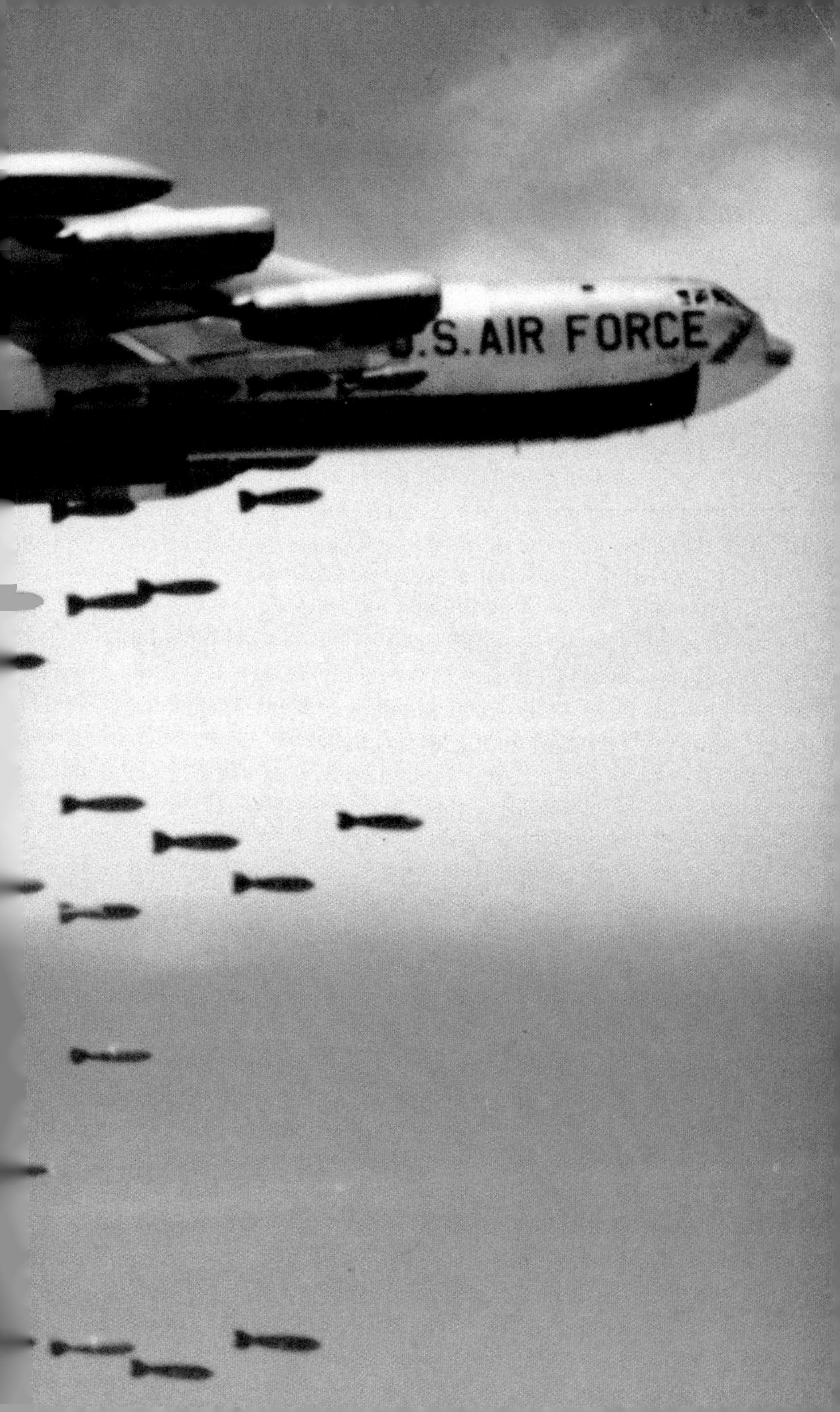
S. AIR FORCE

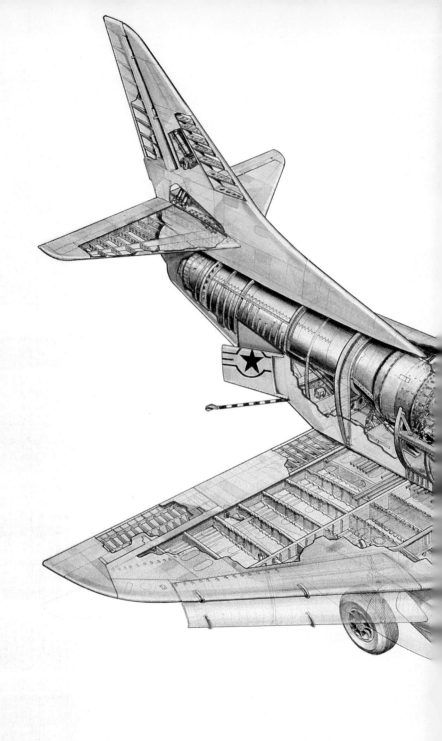

HOT ROD:

Designer Ed Heinemann's classic fighter-bomber, the McDonnell Douglas A-4, is still in service all over the world, but it won its spurs with Navy fliers in Vietnam, building an awesome reputation for maneuverability and ruggedness.

WILD WEASEL:

An F-105G Fairchild Thud adapted for Wild Weasel
electronic countermeasures operations. The two-seat
F-105G was the premier Wild Weasel surface-to-air
missile (SAM) suppression aircraft. Armed with
electronic detection and warning gear plus bombs,
cannon, and radar-homing missiles, the Wild Weasels
knocked out SAM and antiaircraft sites to enable strike
aircraft to reach heavily defended targets in North
Vietnam.

EDITOR IN CHIEF: Ian Ballantine. SERIES EDITORS: Richard Grant, Richard
Ballantine. BOOK EDITOR: John Forbes. PHOTO RESEARCH: John Moore.
DRAWINGS: John Batchelor. MAPS: Peter Williams. PRODUCTION: Owen Watson.
STUDIO: Kim Williams.
PRODUCED BY: The Up & Coming Publishing Company, Bearsville, New York.

STRIKE AIRCRAFT
THE ILLUSTRATED HISTORY OF THE VIETNAM WAR
A Bantam Book / February 1988

ACKNOWLEDGMENTS

*Aircraft nomenclature in this book follows the usual practice of the US
armed services. The aircraft mission is designated by a letter, such as "A"
for Attack, "AC" Attack Cargo (gunship), "B" for Bomber, "F" for
Fighter, "O" for Observation, and "T" for Trainer. The design number is
next, such as B-52. Finally comes the series (or model), such as B-52D or
B-52G. Dates and times are expressed in military terms. Thus, 29 December
1972 at 1800 hours.
I am especially grateful for the assistance rendered by the work of the skilled
and helpful historians at the Naval Historical Center, the History & Museum
Branch, US Marine Corps, and the Air Force's Office of History. They
collect, collate, and compile the historical recod so that others may benefit
from the lessons of history.
If errors appear here, they are inadvertent and my responsibility.
F. Clifton Berry, Jr., Washington, D.C.*

*Photographs for this book were selected from the archives of DAVA, and
Military Archives Research Services.*

Library of Congress Cataloging-in-Publication Data

Berry, F. Clifton, Jr.
    Strike aircraft.

    (The Illustrated history of the Vietnam war)
    1. Vietnamese Conflict, 1961–1975—Aerial operations,
American. 2. Airplanes, Military—United States.
I. Title. II. Series.
DS5558.8.B47   1988   959.704'348   87-27056
ISBN 0-553-34508-7

Published simultaneously in the United States and Canada

PRINTED IN THE UNITED STATES OF AMERICA

CW   0   9   8   7   6   5   4   3   2   1

Contents

Thunder in the air

IN APRIL 1961 General Curtis LeMay, Air Force Chief of Staff, began to take an increased interest in a small and secretive part of the United States Air Force (USAF). It was located at an auxiliary field of Eglin Air Force Base in Florida's panhandle. Hurlburt Field, also known as Eglin Auxiliary Field Number 9, was the base of Tactical Air Command's 4400th Combat Crew Training Squadron.

That name conveys little idea of the unit's purpose. Its nickname, "Jungle Jim," was closer to the mark.

The 4400th was intended to train local air forces in counterinsurgency operations. Its members also expected to conduct air operations themselves if required. In fact, pilots and aircraft from the 4400th flew the first USAF combat mission in South Vietnam.

The unit had less than 350 officers and airmen. All were volunteers, screened for above-average motivation, hardiness, and sense of adventure. Their uniforms followed the nickname: bush hats turned up at the brim, and field fatigue jacket and trousers tucked into boots. They trained in the heat, dust, and humidity of North Florida through the warm spring and steamy summer. Colonel Benjamin H. King was in command.

The conditions approximated those where they would most likely be sent: Southeast Asia.

The Jungle Jim officers and airmen were young and fit, but their aircraft had some years on them. The Jungle Jim fleet comprised sixteen C-47 Gooney Bird transports, eight B-26 Invader bombers, all of World War II or Korean War vintage, and eight T-28 Trojan trainers dating from the early 1950s. All of these were piston-engine, propeller-driven aircraft.

The young air and ground crews, accustomed to

Thunder in the air

READY FOR ACTION: On the flight line at Bien Hoa, a USAF lieutenant and his VNAF back-seater stand in front of a T-28 Nomad with a sample ordnance load, including rocket racks, napalm tanks, and bombs. Vietnam was a military backwater in the early years, and Bien Hoa has the air of an aircraft museum in this February 1963 picture, with World War II vintage B-26s and C-47s on display.

jet fighters and powerful C-130 turboprop transports, adapted quickly to the slower aircraft. Captain Ira L. Kimes, Jr., one of the pilots, recalled, "Where almost all of our people were used to a dive speed of 400 to 500 knots in the Century series fighters like the F-100s and F-104s, we were now down to dive speeds of 200 to 250 knots indicated airspeed." The slower speeds allowed a wider margin for error—or greater accuracy, something that occasionally gave the older aircraft an edge when

supporting troops in close-in combat. The Jungle
Jims earned another nickname about this time: "Air
Commandos." It came from their training program.

They were trained on their newly acquired prop
aircraft to be proficient in flying, shooting, and dropping bombs. They went through a tough survival
school, learning how to live in mountains and jungle,
and received a thorough education in escape and
evasion. A rigorous physical conditioning program
kept them fit through the muggy summer. The unit

Friendly fields —The principal USAF/VNAF airfields in South Vietnam in 1965. Only three, Tan Son Nhut, Da Nang and Bien Hoa, were capable of taking jets.

was ordered to South Vietnam on 11 October 1961, ostensibly for more training; the official word was that is was "not for combat at the present time." The operation was to be called Operation Farmgate.

In mid-November Colonel King led the unit's eight T-28s to Vietnam, landing at Bien Hoa, before flying a short hop to Saigon and back for official clearance.

At Bien Hoa, they encountered a run-down former French airfield. The single runway was made of pierced steel planking that often curled up under hard use. Their living conditions were austere and food and sanitation poor; but then, in theory, they were only in Vietnam on temporary duty.

They were assigned long uncomfortable reconnaissance missions counting sailing junks and sampans in coastal waters. Under the clear Plexiglas canopies of the T-28s, the pilots boiled in the tropical sun.

But the flying was generally good, especially in the early mornings. The big radial engines purred and rumbled, and the land below was interesting and still unfamiliar.

Their mission was unclear, as was the situation in Southeast Asia, where the North Vietnamese, with the backing of Russia and China, were using as yet little-understood guerrilla fighting techniques to undermine the neighboring states of South Vietnam and Laos.

President Kennedy intended the Jungle Jims to perform several functions: as advisers and back-stiffeners for the South Vietnamese Air Force; and as support for the US Army Special Forces people along the borders. Further down the chain of command there were different ideas. General LeMay expected the Air Commandos to conduct combat operations, while at the same time training the Vietnamese. Some of the Joint Chiefs of Staff in Washington and those at Pacific Command in Hawaii favored the combat role. Others wanted to restrict them to training. But everyone from the White House down wanted their presence kept a secret.

As was to happen so often in Vietnam, compromises were made. Operation Farmgate pilots were permitted to fly armed missions as long as they were training a Vietnamese pilot. That seemed a fair

idea, but as the tempo of enemy actions increased, the Vietnamese pilots were needed to fly their own airplanes. That led to the practice of putting any Vietnamese airman into the back seat of a T-28 to satisfy the rules, with the USAF pilot in front flying the mission. The backseaters were accurately nicknamed "sandbags."

Confusion persisted over the limits of the "training" role, and the Joint Chiefs of Staff sent out a directive on 26 December 1961 to make the situation clear: Under Operation Farmgate USAF's Jungle Jims could conduct combat missions only when the Vietnamese Air Force could not.

Events moved faster than the message did. Colonel King had received local authorization to launch an air strike along with the Vietnamese. The targets were Viet Cong houses and rice fields about fifty miles north of Saigon. Captain Kimes recalls: "Up to (then) we had not delivered any ordnance against a target other than on the gunnery range."

In case of need, however, the squadron kept two T-28s on alert during daylight. Machine guns were

Rocket load
—Ground
crewmen arming
T-28s at Bien
Hoa. The T-28s
are still
spotlessly clean,
a month after
arrival in
Vietnam. They
were modified
for combat with
armor at key
points,
especially crew
seats,
gunsights, and a
pair of .50-cal
machine guns.
Ordnance load
was 1,500
pounds—
roughly one-
tenth that of an
F-4.

loaded, the rocket pods armed, and two 500-pound bombs hung on the wings.

Kimes remembers: "My turn (on alert) was on the 26th. Sometime that day I was called in and advised that we had been cleared to go on a combat mission with the South Vietnamese Air Force (VNAF)." The Americans were briefed on the mission along with the South Vietnamese pilots who were to fly the mission in their AD-6s (later called A-1H Skyraiders).

The force took off about noon. Captain Kimes recalls: "I led the Operation Farmgate element, with Captain Rowan on my wing. We proceeded out to a target area with the AD-6s, bombed, strafed, fired our rockets, and returned to the base. As far as I know that was the first combat mission the Air Force flew in South Vietnam." The Joint Chiefs of Staff (JCS) message arrived while the mission was in progress. Radio messages went out to recall the USAF fliers, but too late to stop the first official US combat air strike in Vietnam.

A month and a half later three crewmen, killed when their C-123 transport crashed on a low-level mission from Tan Son Nhut, Saigon, were the first USAF casualties in South Vietnam.

In Washington the administration tried to keep the US involvement quiet while it was drawn gradually but inexorably deeper into the quicksand of Southeast Asia.

Gradually the Farmgate force was expanded and its missions broadened. A simple, austere tactical air control system was installed, and procedures for operating with the Vietnamese forces improved. Navigational aids were still primitive or nonexistent. One Farmgate veteran, Major Frank Gorski, described the procedure: "We just got on the deck and went. If you wanted to get someplace you just picked up a canal and went. That was your navigation system. Flew time and distance. Keep one eye on the fuel and one eye out the window, and press on. Night or day, it didn't make any difference. It was pretty interesting flying, sort of a cross (between) an old-time mail pilot and modern-day aviator."

Through 1962 and 1963 the Vietnamese conflict expanded, and more US Air Force training, reconnaissance, and transport aircraft were sent in. US

Thunder in the air

SECURITY ALERT:
Jungle Jims'
commander Col.
Benjamin King
(left) and a
colleague study
a map of Bien
Hoa air base,
checking its
vulnerability to
Viet Cong
attacks. During
the second
month of USAF
deployment in
Vietnam the
base was placed
on alert—after
an attack.

23

Thunder in the air

ESCORT DUTY: A T-28 "flying shotgun" over a supply train rolling through jungle southeast of Bien Hoa, early in 1963. Four bombs and two tanks of napalm were adequate to help ground troops deal with most ambushes encountered at this time. The ordnance was delivered with an accuracy that could only be offered by the slow-maneuverable Nomad.

Army helicopter units also flowed into the country. In the summer of 1963 the Farmgate force at Bien Hoa became the 1st Air Commando Squadron (Composite), a regular organization. Its fleet expanded to 42 aircraft, but still the same three basic types: C-47, T-28, and B-26.

By March 1964, after a succession of military coups and internal power struggles, the South Vietnamese war effort was in turmoil, and the

Communists were stepping up attacks. The Joint
Chiefs of Staff proposed military action against
North Vietnam, beginning with reconnaissance
flights over neighboring Laos and North Vietnam.
After that, full-scale air and naval air operations
would commence if the president, by now Lyndon
B. Johnson, wished. LBJ withheld a decision while
Secretary of Defense Robert McNamara, Secretary
of State Dean Rusk, and other senior officials

assessed the situation and recommended options. Eventually, the consensus of LBJ's top advisers was to wait and see.

However, among other low-key operations, the president did order air and sea reconnaissance of the North. That included reconnaissance of the coastline by US Navy destroyers. The first ship so committed was the USS *Maddox*, which on 28 July 1964 moved through the Gulf of Tonkin to sail within thirty miles of shore to collect information and show the flag. The North Vietnamese did not take long to react. On the afternoon of 2 August, North Vietnamese patrol boats shadowing the *Maddox* reportedly fired at the destroyer in international waters, but without inflicting damage. Two nights later a similar attack was reported on the Maddox and another destroyer, the *C. Turner Joy*.

Interpreting these as a series of provocative acts, Washington decided that they required a definite response. Johnson ordered the execution of preplanned air strikes against North Vietnam for first light on 5 August. The strike aircraft were to be Navy, launched from the carriers USS *Ticonderoga* and USS *Constellation*.

At first light, their flight deck launch catapults went into action, propelling 64 strike aircraft skyward to North Vietnam. The 64 included A-1 Skyraiders, and jet-powered A-4 Skyhawks and F-8

Crusaders. Their targets: the North Vietnamese gunboat and torpedo boat fleet bases on the coast.

While the aircraft streaked toward their targets, President Johnson prepared to speak on radio and television. He spoke as the first strikes were hitting. He said the US response to the hostile actions by North Vietnam were "limited and fitting." The Navy air strikes hit the patrol boat bases and fuel depots. Sixty-two aircraft returned. Two were lost. The pilot of one of those aircraft, an A-4 Skyhawk, bailed out over North Vietnam. Lieutenant (j.g.) Everett Alvarez from the *Constellation* became the first aviator to be taken prisoner of war. He remained a POW for eight and one-half years.

LBJ asked Congress for authority to take necessary action. By the 7th of August he had it, in the Gulf of Tonkin resolution. It not only approved retaliatory attacks but also gave the president an open account to take measures and steps he might determine, including the use of armed force, in Southeast Asia. The die was cast.

Both sides began quickly to escalate the conflict. Two days after the boat bases were hit, thirty-nine MiG-15 and MiG-17 fighters supplied by China arrived at the Phuc Yen airfield near Hanoi. More fighters reinforced bases in South China and on Hainan Island, off the North Vietnamese coast.

General Hunter Harris, commander of Pacific Air Forces (PACAF), recommended an immediate attack on Phuc Yen to destroy the MiGs. F-105 Thunderchiefs newly based at Korat in Thailand could do the job.

Washington refused. But LBJ called for additional forces to move into Southeast Asia. They were to include USAF jets from regular units, not converted trainers.

F-102 interceptors flew into Da Nang and Tan Son Nhut. F-100 Super Sabre fighters landed at Da Nang and Takhli. B-57 Canberra medium bombers, already poised at Clark Air Base (AB) in the Philippines, moved forward to Bien Hoa. Eight F-105s had already arrived at Korat in Thailand. RF-101 reconnaissance and KB-50 refueling aircraft also flew into South Vietnam. Other aircraft from the States were staged across the Pacific at bases in the Philippines and Okinawa, poised in readiness for Vietnam service. For the remainder of 1964 the US buildup

Near miss —An RB-57 reconnaissance jet unscathed by a rocket round that landed a few yards away during a Viet Cong attack on Tan Son Nhut air base, near Saigon. The blast walls and steel fencing between aircraft were to stop explosions spreading and limit the damage caused by bomb fragments among the tightly packed aircraft.

continued. The number of aircraft of all US services increased from 388 aircraft at the beginning of the year (including 248 helicopters) to 561 (including 327 helicopters).

North Vietnam built up its forces too. After Premier Pham Van Dong visited Moscow in November 1964, Soviet assistance was obtained to build up a modern air defense system. Surface-to-air missiles (SAMs), heavy antiaircraft guns, and their controlling radar and radio systems began to arrive soon after.

The Viet Cong guerrillas operating in South

Thunder in the air

SMOKY JOE:
Explosive cartridges start the twin jets of one of the first B-57 Canberras in Vietnam. The British-designed light bomber was sent to South Vietnam in 1964 as part of the US response to the Gulf of Tonkin attacks, and was a workhorse in the early years of the conflict. As antiaircraft defenses improved and the conflict intensified the Canberra proved too vulnerable for day operations. Modified versions with infrared sensors flew night interdiction missions until the US withdrawal in 1972.

Vietnam were also rearmed throughout 1964. General William C. Westmoreland, commander of US forces in Vietnam from 1965 to 1968, reported that after the Gulf of Tonkin incidents they received "progressively larger and more modern weapons, including heavy mortars, rockets, and antiaircraft weapons." US air bases provided them with targets that combined vulnerability and high value.

At Bien Hoa on the night of 1 November 1964, Viet Cong mortar units got through the weak Vietnamese defenses, and within thirty minutes their shelling killed 4 Americans and wounded 72. Two

Delicate job
—American
ground
crewmen screw
the fuzes into
100-pound
bombs on a
VNAF A-1E
Skyraider at
Bien Hoa. The
fuzes contain
explosive
detonators that
trigger the main
charge on
impact or,
depending on
the type of fuze,
at a set time
after release or
impact. Once
the fuzes were
set and the
bombs armed,
the rule was
that they could
not be
unloaded, to
avoid flight-line
disasters.

Vietnamese were killed and 5 wounded. The mortar barrage destroyed five USAF B-57 bombers and one H-43 helicopter, and damaged thirteen B-57s and three H-43s. VNAF lost three A-1s destroyed and three more Skyraiders plus two C-47s damaged.

The attack came at the end of the 1964 presidential election campaign. With the Republican challenger Senator Barry Goldwater being portrayed as a warmonger by the Democrats, President Johnson, who was to be reelected by a landslide, delayed deciding how best to retaliate.

In December, with the election out of the way, he ordered more covert actions against North Vietnam, air strikes on the infiltration routes in Laos, and reprisal bombing if warranted. At some unspecified future time, air strikes would begin against infiltration targets north of the Demilitarized Zone. Then if the North Vietnamese did not "show restraint," the strikes by both USAF and Navy aircraft would eventually creep northward to the 19th Parallel. (Hanoi is at the 21st Parallel.)

The air strike campaign in Laos against the infiltration routes was given the name Barrel Roll. The very restricted campaign was to be run from Washington. Two missions of four strike aircraft would be flown each week. The targets were selected at the National Security Council. Infiltration route segments were designated for armed reconnaissance. Fixed targets, often road bridges which were hard to hit and easily repaired, were selected to be hit with ordnance remaining aboard after the armed sweep was finished. This was air power by remote micromanagement. Its cost was high and the results small.

If Barrel Roll was intended to send a clear signal to North Vietnam, the message did not get through. Its leaders were unimpressed. Instead regular regiments of the North Vietnamese Army (NVA) began appearing in the South beginning in December 1964.

Attacks on US installations became heavier, provoking increasingly heavy responses against NVA barracks complexes by US and South Vietnamese planes, in air strikes designated Flaming Dart I and II. These in turn stimulated retaliatory guerrilla raids until, after the last Flaming Dart strike of 11 February 1965, American dependents were

Scorched concrete and smouldering aircraft dot the flightline at Bien Hoa after an accidental explosion triggered off a chain reaction among aircraft loaded with fuel and high explosives, early in 1965. Accidents like this one, and increasingly frequent Viet Cong mortar and rocket attacks, soon produced improvements in safety procedures.

evacuated from South Vietnam and additional aircraft resources were flown into South Vietnam and Thailand.

The commander-in-chief Pacific (CINCPAC), Admiral Ulysses S. Grant Sharp, and General Westmoreland were preparing to lay on air strikes against North Vietnam. They wanted to be ready for possible reactions by North Vietnam and Communist China.

Westmoreland ordered the first openly acknowledged USAF mission in South Vietnam on 19 February 1965. Four B-57 Canberra bombers from Bien Hoa bombed VC base camps in Phuoc Tuy Province outside Saigon. They struck again during the period from 21 to 24 February.

On 19 February, in the central highlands, Westmoreland used emergency authority to commit USAF jet aircraft in an all-American relief effort. Army UH-1 helicopters flew into the An Khe valley to rescue 220 troops surrounded by a regular NVA battalion. Covering air strikes were flown by F-100s, B-57s, and A-1Es.

By now it was obvious that unless LBJ was prepared to lose South Vietnam, US involvement had to expand. The North would have to be struck more heavily and regularly, not as in Barrel Roll and Flaming Dart. US aircraft would have to be

NEW ARRIVALS:
F-100 Supersabres roll out of formation over Saigon in 1965. On February 8, F-100s escorted the first raid on North Vietnam in Operation Flaming Dart. The finned drop tanks could be used in supersonic flight.

used openly in both North and South Vietnam. Commitment of US troops to the fight in the South might be required.

In March 1965 a bombing campaign against North Vietnam began, combat air operations in the south were given full authorization, and the Marines went ashore at Da Nang.

On 2 March air strikes against the North started the Rolling Thunder campaign. It was described by Admiral Sharp as "a precise application of military pressure for the specific purpose of halting aggression in South Vietnam." Rolling Thunder was to begin with air strikes on military targets just north of the Demilitarized Zone (DMZ). The strikes would roll northward to the 19th Parallel. North Vietnamese reaction would be assessed. If the North

Vietnamese continued to press the war in the South, Rolling Thunder strikes would edge northward to the 20th Parallel, just 60 miles south of Hanoi. Later, if necessary, military targets north of the 20th Parallel would be hit. The idea was that the North Vietnamese would cease aggression in the South and come to the bargaining table rather than suffer the consequences of a bombing campaign.

The first strike in Rolling Thunder was carried out by 25 USAF F-105s and 20 B-57s based in South Vietnam. They hit an ammunition storage site at Xom Bong, between the DMZ and Dong Hoi.

For aircrews of the Air Force, Marines, and Navy flying strike missions, the scope of operations had widened and the hazards increased. Thunder was in the air and on the ground.

Dragon's jaw

ROLLING THUNDER lasted for more than three years, from 1965 to 1968.

But it was not intended to last that long by those who devised it. The field commanders and Joint Chiefs of Staff favored a short, sharp campaign of near-simultaneous attacks on 94 key points such as bridges, fuel stores, communications centers, rail yards, and ports. They should be struck concurrently with the full force of Air Force and Navy strike aircraft. That way, the defenses would be overwhelmed. USAF Chief General John P. McConnell advocated a high-pressure 28-day campaign.

However, it began much more modestly, under tight restrictions from Washington.

In April 1965, 1,500 Rolling Thunder sorties were flown against the North by Air Force and Navy aviation strike aircraft. The 50 daily sorties were split about evenly between Air Force and Naval aviation. The strikes were kept below the 20th Parallel. At the same time, an intensified series of strikes against the Communist infiltration routes, called Steel Tiger, began in the panhandle of southern Laos.

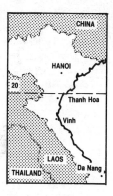

Rolling Thunder immediately highlighted the importance of key choke points in North Vietnam, which were to be the focus of some epic air battles. South of the 20th Parallel, destruction of five railroad bridges and the rail yard at Vinh would immobilize the 115-mile rail system from Vinh to the DMZ. To trap as much rail stock as possible south of the 20th Parallel, only two bridges needed to be downed: the Dang Phuong rail and highway bridge, and the Thanh Hoa bridge. To choke four of the five rail lines in Vietnam, and to block highway traffic in and out of Hanoi, only one bridge needed to be

Lt. Col. Rob Risner —Commanded the first strikes on the Thanh Hoa bridge in April 1965. One of the more famous airmen in the Vietnam War, he was already an ace from the Korean War. Risner led the 67th TFS, based in Korat, Thailand. He was awarded the Air Force Cross for his courage and leadership during the attacks on Thanh Hoa. Shot down by a ground-to-air missile ten miles north of Thanh Hoa in September 1965, he was held as a POW for more than seven years.

downed: the Paul Doumer bridge on the outskirts of the North Vietnamese capital.

For the moment, the Paul Doumer bridge was in the Hanoi sanctuary zone specified by Washington, and could not be struck. But the massive Thanh Hoa bridge over the Song Ma River, 76 miles south of Hanoi, was at the top of the target list. It was known by the Vietnamese as Ham Rong—"the Dragon's Jaw."

The first strike against the Thanh Hoa bridge was set for 2 April 1965, but bad weather delayed it until the next day. The mission was assigned to the F-105D Thunderchiefs of 67th Tactical Fighter Squadron (TFS). The strike was led by Lieutenant Colonel Robinson Risner, an ace from the Korean War, and commander of the 67th TFS, based at Korat, Thailand. Risner was one of the Air Force's most skilled and respected fighter leaders.

Colonel Risner's squadron (nicknamed "The Fighting Cocks") was the nucleus of the 79 aircraft assembled for the first strike on Thanh Hoa bridge. Forty-six were F-105s. There were 10 converted transports, KC-135s, for refueling, 21 F-100s for high cover against MiGs, and 2 RF-101s for pre- and post-strike aerial photography.

Seven of the F-100s would fly flak suppression. Of the F-105s, 15, loaded with eight 750-pound bombs each, would also suppress the flak. The other 31 would hit the bridge itself, 16 with two Bullpup missiles, the rest with a conventional load of 750-pound bombs.

The plan was to strike the abutments at both ends of the bridge in a rapid succession of attack passes by flights of four aircraft. They would take off in sequence from temporary bases at Takhli and Korat in Thailand, be refueled over the Mekong River, then dash across Laos into North Vietnam.

The strike worked as planned. When it was finished ten dozen bombs and 32 missiles had been aimed at the Thanh Hoa bridge. But as the smoke and dust cleared for the waiting reconnaissance planes, it was clear that damage was superficial.

Two aircraft were lost to the flak, which was more intense than anticipated. Colonel Risner's F-105 was hit and damaged, but he nursed it back to safety at Da Nang.

Another strike against the bridge was ordered for

the next day, 4 April. Colonel Risner led again but the ineffective Bullpups were omitted. Instead, 48 F-105s would each drop eight 750-pound general purpose bombs on the bridge. No flak suppression aircraft were scheduled, although F-100s would fly high cover against MiGs.

Weather conditions were low clouds and haze, so the strikes were flown from east to west, heading inland instead of out to sea. Time over target was 1100. Robbie Risner hit the initial point on the mark at 1057, then headed north, leading the bombing force against the Dragon's Jaw again. He was ordered to remain high and direct the strike, so Captain Smitty Harris was the first man "down the chute."

Harris rolled in at a steep dive angle, releasing his bombs at 4,000 feet. He pulled out at 1,000 feet and began a turn to the east toward the sea, and safety. The 37mm flak reached up and hit his aircraft hard. His engine was out, his left fuel tank had blown off, and his aft fuselage was burning. The other pilots yelled at him over the radio to get out. But he could not hear them. His radio was shot out. Harris fought to get the aircraft under control so he could make it to the sea, only ten miles away. But

DRAGON'S JAW: The Thanh Hoa bridge is partially obscured by cloud shadow in this aerial photo. The first Thanh Hoa bridge was built by the French and destroyed by the Communist Viet Minh. Later, the North Vietnamese rebuilt the combined rail-highway bridge to a stronger specification, with aid from the Chinese.

THUNDERCHIEF:
The stencils on the cockpit flank of this F-105D indicate 25 completed missions. Nicknamed the "Thud"— sarcastically at first—the F-105 won the loyalty of airmen in Vietnam.

the fire spread and within minutes he was flying a chunk of flaming metal. He had no choice but to bail out. He ejected, descended to the ground, and was immediately captured. Smitty Harris spent nearly eight years as a prisoner of war.

Risner's other 46 F-105s pressed the attack without mishap, until the last strike flight got ahead of schedule, and circled overhead to await their turn at the target.

As they circled, four MiG-17s darted out of the clouds in a diving, high-speed pass. This was a first. The MiGs had not risen before to challenge the strike aircraft. They swooped down on the flight leader and his wingman from behind, killing them

both, then dashed out of the area at top speed. This first MiG attack meant a new threat had materialized rapidly: enemy interceptors under accurate ground control. Also, heavier caliber 57mm flak had been identified on this strike. Suddenly the sky over North Vietnam had become a much more dangerous place.

Almost 350 bombs were aimed at the bridge on this second attack. Three hundred of them hit it, but the bridge was still in place. It was damaged, and needed extensive repairs, but it was now obvious that the Thanh Hoa bridge was much sturdier than other bridges in North Vietnam. The others were being knocked out readily by the 750-pound bombs,

Bridges down —The Rolling Thunder campaign quickly dropped most of the important bridges in North Vietnam, as these pictures show. The North Vietnamese responded in various ways. Ferries and temporary pontoon bridges were set up while repair work went on, and materiel surged southward during the various bombing pauses.

which were evidently not big enough to knock out the Thanh Hoa bridge completely.

The Air Force evaluated the two strikes and the enemy's increasingly strong defenses. Tactics were revised and planning improved, especially with respect to MiG cover. The F-100 was inadequate against the multiple threats in the North. The F-4C Phantom was far superior, and was beginning to show up in the war theater. (The first Phantom squadron of the US Marines, F-4Bs of VMFA-531, arrived at Da Nang on 10 April 1965.)

The North Vietnamese put an all-out effort into making the bridge usable. It was ready for rail traffic in early May, just a month after the previous strike, so the Thuds, as the F-100s were nicknamed, returned to hit it again in a cycle of destruction and repair that seemed destined to continue indefinitely.

On 12 May, President Johnson ordered a pause in Rolling Thunder. The object: to observe North Vietnamese response to the peaceful gesture implicit in the bombing pause. North Vietnam made no peace moves. Within four days, reconnaissance flights showed that North Vietnam was simply taking advantage of the respite to surge supplies southward.

CINCPAC and the Joint Chiefs now recommended that armed reconnaissance sweeps be permitted north of the 20th Parallel, and against specific ports and military installations in the sanctuary around Hanoi and Haiphong. But Washington prohibited such widening of the strikes, fearing that China would enter the war.

So Rolling Thunder continued south of the 20th Parallel. But continued poor visibility and adverse weather meant that in some months only four days were good enough for precise strikes. Also, most of the fixed targets below 20° North had already been hit. The North Vietnamese countered the destruction of railway lines and bridges by moving more supplies at night and on trucks. They understood keenly the Americans' self-imposed rules of engagement and exploited them to the full by parking their trucks in villages during the day, making them immune to air strikes.

The Thanh Hoa bridge was now in a strike area, known as "Route Pack IV," assigned to the US Navy. From June 1965 until the bombing halt of 1968, Navy and Marine strike aircraft flew almost

700 sorties against the bridge. The results were always the same: The bridge was closed to traffic temporarily, but reopened in due course. So many bomb and missile craters pocked the approaches that the areas on both ends were called "the Valley of the Moon."

By mid-1965, the North Vietnamese Air Force had seventy MiG-17 interceptors. They were not often launched against strike forces. However, they trained intensively in the northern sanctuary area, and would pop up from time to time to engage a strike, usually against bomb-laden F-105s.

When the MiG-17s did engage in aerial combat with the Navy F-4B and Air Force F-4C Phantoms, they lost. Two Navy F-4Bs destroyed two MiG-17s with Sparrow air-to-air missiles on 17 June.

Three weeks later, on 10 July, USAF F-4Cs of the 45th Tactical Fighter Squadron at Ubon, Thailand, tricked the MiGs from Phuc Yen northeast of

Dragon's jaw

RELEASE POINT:
The jagged silhouette of the F-105 is perfectly outlined against a cloud base in this picture of a radar bombing mission over North Vietnam. The odd plane out is an RB-66 Destroyer, which is using its electronic navigation gear to control the Thuds' bombing run. The bombs are 3,000-pounders.

Hanoi. The MiGs usually waited to intercept until a strike was over and the Phantom escorts were low on fuel. This time, a Phantom flight of four came over the target fifteen minutes late, flying at speeds and altitudes that emulated loaded F-105s. The MiGs took the bait. In the ensuing melee, two of the F-4C crews got two MiG-17s with Sidewinder infrared homing missiles.

These were the first Navy and Air Force MiG kills. More would come, but in the meantime the MiGs

avoided a fight. From 10 July through March 1966, they continued training and perfecting ground-controlled intercept (GCI) procedures. It was clear, however, that North Vietnam was developing from scratch a potent and integrated air defense force.

Another element of the defenses was just being moved into place.

The first identified site of the SA-2 Guideline ground-to-air missile was detected by a Navy RF-8A Crusader from the USS *Coral Sea* on 5 April 1965,

Thud Ridge —The F-105's nickname was tagged onto a piece of key terrain in North Vietnam. "Thud Ridge" was the name given to a prominent mountain range used as a landmark by aviators striking the North. It began about 20 miles northwest of Hanoi, rising to more than 5,000 feet as it extended further northwest. Unmistakable by eye or on radar, Thud Ridge was used for navigation and target orientation. The Phuc Yen jet base sat between Thud Ridge and Hanoi, while the Thai Nguyen industrial complex lay a few miles to the east.

15 miles southeast of Hanoi. Air Force and Navy leaders recommended immediate destruction of the site. Permission was denied. Another site under construction was detected a month later. By mid-July 1965, several more sites in various stages of readiness had been found in a ring around Hanoi. No missiles were at the sites.

That changed on 24 July 1965. On that day, two SA-2s were launched at a flight of four Air Force F-4C Phantoms. One aircraft was lost and the other three damaged. Four F-105s hit a SAM site four days later. In August, SAMs killed two Navy A-4 Skyhawks from the USS *Midway*. Again, permission was sought to strike SAM sites. This time, it was given. The sites were usually camouflaged, and many dummy installations were built. Since the missiles and radar were mobile, a loaded site could quickly be emptied or an empty site made ready. Some time passed before the first Navy SAM strike was made on 17 October, by Navy A-4E Skyhawks from USS *Independence*. That was near Kep airfield, forty miles northeast of Hanoi.

Pilots soon realized they could dodge the SA-2. Its launch produced a cloud of smoke and dust. If they could spot that cloud and the distinctive "telephone pole" rising out of it, they could outmaneuver the missile. Also, the FAN SONG radar emissions could be detected on a radar warning receiver and converted to recognizable tones in aircrew headsets. Variations in the tones told when a missile was launched. Finally, both the radar and the radio guidance could be jammed, if electronic warfare aircraft were on hand.

President Johnson halted Rolling Thunder on Christmas Day 1965. He tried again to bring Hanoi to the conference table. The bombing pause lasted for 37 days, through 30 January 1966. During the respite, Hanoi once again repaired damage and surged men and materials to the war in South Vietnam. Rolling Thunder resumed on 31 March for two months, through February and March, still under tight White House control. The Navy and Air Force were restricted to lower North Vietnam, and limited to a joint total of 300 sorties daily.

When the Johnson Administration reached an "essential understanding" with North Vietnam in the 1968 Paris peace talks, LBJ decided to end all

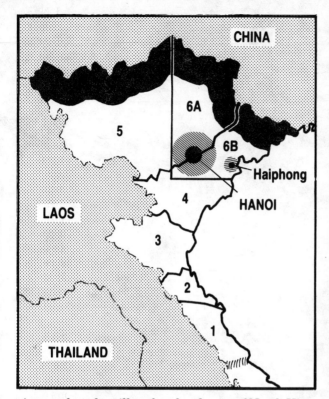

CHINA

6A

5

6B

Haiphong

4

HANOI

LAOS

3

2

1

THAILAND

ROUTE PACKAGES:
As the air war became more complex, a system was devised to avoid duplication of effort. CINCPAC divided North Vietnam into seven areas, called "route packages," each assigned to Air Force or Navy. The responsible service gathered intelligence information and was primarily responsible for strikes in its sectors. The map also shows sanctuary areas around Hanoi and Haiphong where no strikes were permitted. There was also a 30-mile buffer zone along the Chinese border.

air, naval, and artillery bombardment of North Vietnam. He announced on 31 October that the bombardment would cease effective at 0800 on 1 November, 1968, Washington time. That was the end of Rolling Thunder.

The last strike was actually flown an hour and a half before Johnson announced the halt, by Major Frank Lenahan of the 8th Tactical Fighter Wing based at Ubon, Thailand. He and his backseater in an F-4D struck a target near Dong Hoi, not far from where the first Rolling Thunder strikes were flown three years and nine months earlier.

During Rolling Thunder, tactical strike aircraft of the Air Force, Navy, and Marines flew 304,000 sorties against the North. The Strategic Air Command's B-52s flew 2,380. Together, they dropped more than 643,000 tons of bombs on Vietnam. More than nine hundred fixed-wing aircraft were lost over North Vietnam in that period. And more than five hundred US airmen had become POWs, forced to endure the conditions of Hanoi's POW camps.

Rescue at A Shau

THROUGHOUT 1966 in the South, the US troop buildup continued, only to be matched by the enemy, who kept pace both in quantity and in quality of equipment. Regular NVA divisions were now in the northern provinces of South Vietnam. NVA regiments and main force VC units kept up attacks against remote Special Forces camps along the entire border throughout the year. One of the most serious attacks occurred at A Shau in March.

The A Shau valley lies due west of Da Nang in the remote and high Annamite chain of mountains smack on the infiltration route from North Vietnam through Laos and into the northern provinces of South Vietnam.

The camp was one of those whose mission was to block infiltration and watch the border with Laos. The A Shau camp comprised a fortified compound, a 2,500-foot assault airstrip capable of taking C-47 and C-123 transports, and an area cleared all around and sown with land mines.

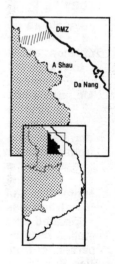

In response to intelligence findings, the garrison was reinforced in early March. By Tuesday, 8 March 1966, the camp was defended by 220 Vietnamese of the Civilian Irregular Defense Group (CIDG), ten men from the US Special Forces, six from the Vietnamese Special Forces, and 41 civilians.

Two regular NVA regiments, the 95B and 101C, began probing the outer defenses of the A Shau camp on the evening of 8 March. Early on the 9th they opened up with heavy mortar barrages. Heavy ground fog hampered air strikes.

The northeast monsoon was still bringing rainclouds. From November until April, the monsoon imposed perpetual low cloud ceilings and overcast over North Vietnam and the northern part

READY TO ROLL: Skyraiders on the tarmac at Qui Nhon, about to taxi to the runway. Mountains and unreliable weather made flying hazardous from all the air bases in the Central Highlands. Qui Nhon was operated as a satellite base by personnel from Bien Hoa to cut flying time for air support missions, which were usually close by and were called at short notice.

of South Vietnam. The A Shau valley was invisible from cruising altitude.

No artillery was available to support the camp. Air strikes were the only outside fire support. During the day on the 9th, A-1 "Sandy" Skyraiders and AC-47 gunships made repeated attempts to strike the attackers. One of the AC-47s was shot down. It was destroyed by friendly aircraft to keep its guns and radios from the enemy. At Da Nang, the camp was thought to be lost. But its defenders held out, squeezed into one corner.

A-1Es that were already in the air and headed for preplanned targets were diverted to A Shau early on 10 March. One flight of two aircraft was led by Major Bernard F. Fisher whose unit was based at Pleiku. His wingman was Captain Francisco "Paco" Vazquez. Another two-aircraft A-1 flight was led by Major Dafford W. "Jump" Myers, based at Qui Nhon.

Bernie Fisher hunted around above the cloud layer until he recognized intersecting canyons that were about ten miles northwest of the camp. Knowing his location, Fisher was ready to penetrate the clouds and fly down into the A Shau valley. Major Myers' flight arrived about the same time, and slotted in behind them.

Two more A-1s arrived about then, flown by

captains Lucas and Hague. Fisher had them fly down through the cloud base by homing on his radio transmissions.

Fisher describes the scene: "We went down in on the valley floor. The mountains were still quite obscured. There was maneuver room, but not much room for bombing." The valley was about a mile wide and six miles long. The pilots nicknamed it "the tube." The overcast was below the tops of the hills around the valley, forcing the A-1s to operate amidst ground fire from all directions, including some guns higher on the hills than the aircraft. One pilot later described it as "like flying inside Yankee Stadium with the people in the bleachers firing at you with machine guns."

More aircraft, jets with heavy loads, arrived over the scene. But they could not be vectored through the overcast onto the targets. Fisher's A-1s were the only ones who could help.

"We flew right on the deck. We crossed over the AC-47 we had destroyed the day before. We could see smoke coming out of a little fort ahead of us. The visibility was pretty good." Fisher contacted the defenders on an Army FM radio to offer help and learn the situation. One of the Americans in the fort responded. Fisher continues: "He advised us that the camp had been overrun. The enemy occupied

BELEAGUERED CAMP:
The Special Forces base at A Shau. The battle for the camp centered on the triangular compound toward the top of the picture. Major Myers put down on the strip in the foreground. This reconnaissance picture is printed in negative, which produces an impression of upside-down perspective.

ROLL OF HONOR: Major Bernard Fisher unsticking his A-1E from Pleiku with a load of 72 100-pound antipersonnel bombs, and a belly tank.

everything except the communications bunker and the north bunker. We were cleared to hit anything in the camp except those areas."

Fisher set up his first four A-1s for strafing passes. They could only attack in one direction, straight down the valley, fire their cannon, make a hard left 180-degree turn, and fly back up the valley for the next pass. Fisher led the first pass. "We set up and rolled in and strafed the south wall. You could see a lot of the people down there, a lot of them moving

around, and a lot laying on the ground. We could see the weapons that some of them had in their hands just for a moment. They wore uniforms, had helmets on."

The NVA gunners soon found the range. Their gunfire riddled the windscreen of Captain Hubert King's aircraft. He could not see, and was forced to climb out through the overcast to return to base.

Fisher led the remaining three aircraft on a second strafing pass down the valley. On that pass, Jump

A-1 Skyraider Douglas USAF, USN, VNAF —Navy dive bomber first flown in 1945. Also used by USAF and VNAF. The E model had two seats; the H model, one. Up to 8,000 pounds of bombs could be carried for close support missions. The A-1 carried enough fuel for up to four hours without refuelling. It was a favorite close air support aircraft during the entire conflict: maneuverable, heavy bomb load, four 20-mm cannon, and long endurance.

Myers was hit. He felt the aircraft lurch. He remembered, "I've been hit by .50-caliber before, but this was something bigger, maybe the Chinese 37mm cannon. Almost immediately the engine started sputtering and cutting out, and then it conked out for good."

Myers had no choice but to try for the airstrip, even though it was controlled by the enemy and covered by heavy guns. Smoke and flames blocked his forward vision, so Bernie Fisher talked him through the approach. At the last moment he called for him to jerk up his landing gear to avoid sliding off the strip. But as Myers touched down, the belly fuel tank blew up.

Fisher watched the crash. "A huge ball of flame went up and the fuel spilled and it followed him right to where he stopped. He skidded several hundred feet, then slid off to the right side of the runway. The flames followed him down and caught up with him and he went into a huge ball of fire. I thought he would get out. Usually you can get right out and run, but he didn't. It seemed like an awfully long while. We estimated about 40 seconds because I made almost a 270-degree turn around him in a bank."

Bernie Fisher notified the control aircraft high above that Myers was down, probably hurt and trapped inside the airplane. He continued his turn all around the valley, and then spotted Myers coming out. "He looked like he was burning. There was smoke coming off him, but I guess it was because he was saturated with smoke in the cockpit. He ran down the wing, jumped off, and ran a short distance."

Myers rolled into the brush and hid along an embankment by the edge of the strip. Fisher saw him run and hide. "I dove right at him. When I went over him he looked up and saw me and waved. So I knew he was in pretty good shape, but I thought he was burned badly." Fisher called the control aircraft for a rescue helicopter for Myers. They said it would take at least twenty minutes to arrive. Ten minutes later they called to say it was still twenty minutes away.

Captains Lucas and Hague in the other A-1 flight had arrived in "the Tube." These two, Fisher and Paco, began strafing cover over Myers. "We had to

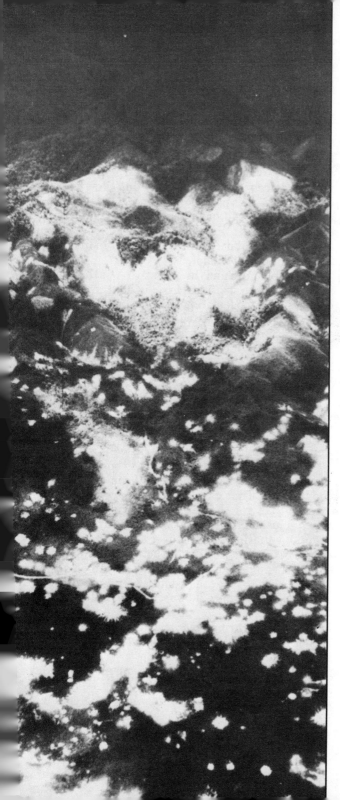

Rescue at A Shau

MOONSCAPE: The trail running through the A Shau valley is dappled with sunlight and pocked with bomb craters, which show white with the reflection from the water lying in them. The heavily blasted section in the center of the picture is where an NVA truck park was hit by B-52s.

Ground support —Bernie Fisher (right) checks out his survival compass with his ground crew chief Tech Sgt. Rodney L. J. Souza. Fisher paid tribute to Souza after A Shau: "I'm sure had we not had the airplane in such good condition we would have damaged it more. . . . I can't speak highly enough of him."

strafe over the top of him and into the wall so the ricochets wouldn't hit him. We were down to fifty to one hundred feet, almost level strafing to keep their heads down."

Fisher knew that if he left the scene to go up to meet the rescue helicopter the enemy would get Myers. "They'd have got him. They were all over the place. He was pretty well concealed in the brush there." Fisher decided he would land to pick up Myers. He told the command post airplane, and they tried to discourage him. Fisher said, "You've got to do it because he's part of the family. One of our people. You know you have to get him out. I felt confident we could get him out of there." His courageous execution of that decision was to result in his receiving the Medal of Honor.

Fisher told Paco and the other two A-1s to give him support, to keep strafing. He set up for the approach, but was a bit too fast. Smoke concealed the runway. He kept power on to fly through the smoke and see what was on the other side. He was going too fast to stop, although he touched his wheels. He poured power to the engine, and pulled up to one hundred feet for another attempt.

Fisher stayed below one hundred feet and executed a tight 180. The enemy fire kept reaching for him. He landed downwind, but had a clearer view of the strip. He touched down just where he wanted to be, and began rolling down the strip.

"It didn't look like I was going to be able to stop. I just rode the brakes as hard as I could and pulled the flaps up. That gave a little more weight on the brakes." He got the airplane stopped on the dirt overrun just off the far end of the runway. He turned around, wingtip swinging over the top of 55-gallon drums in the dirt, and the tail actually bumping one.

"So I swung around in the dirt and came back on the runway." Fisher taxied fast, looking for Myers. "I knew about where he was, and when I taxied by him he was there. He was still crouched down, and he waved both arms vigorously as I went by him." Fisher hit the brakes, but he was still rolling so fast it took one hundred feet to stop.

He stopped, expecting Myers to run alongside and jump in. Myers wasn't there. "So I figured he must be hurt more than I thought. Maybe he couldn't move. So I set the brakes on the bird and was going to jump out and give him a hand to get in. I climbed over the right seat to get out the side he was on. I looked through the mirror and saw two red beady eyes trying to crawl up the back end of the wing. He said I had the power too high. Maybe I did; I thought I had it back to idle, but he might have been a little bit tired, too. But he said that was the fastest dash an old man has ever made, that hundred feet. (Myers was 46.)

"He got up on the wing and got his head inside. I grabbed him by the seat of the pants and pulled him head first right into the floor of the airplane. It was hard on his head but he didn't complain."

The enemy gunners hit the aircraft three times while Fisher was sitting there. "It sounds like hitting your hand against a tin building, banging it real hard. It is obvious, you can tell you're hit."

The three other A-1s had kept on bombing and strafing, even though Lucas's plane was damaged. They were out of ammunition by the time Fisher pulled Myers on board. They made another low pass to keep the enemy down, Lucas saying later, "They didn't know we were out of ordnance!"

Fisher got Myers sorted out and settled in the right-hand seat. Fisher got back into his seat and turned the aircraft around. He jammed the throttle

TOUGH SHIP: The A-1 Skyraider, which played the lead role in the drama at A Shau, could take a lot of punishment, as this shot of an A-1E hit by ground fire shows. The aircraft's other outstanding characteristic was its flight endurance, which in theory could be as long as 12 hours. The A-1 was ideal for escorting rescue helicopters.

forward for maximum power. The big A-1 began rolling down the strip dodging garbage and building airspeed. The gunners not being strafed by his companions were trying to knock Fisher down. (Nineteen hits were counted when he got the airplane back to base at Pleiku.) The aircraft was low on fuel and all its ordnance was gone, so it was relatively light.

Fisher said, "We pressed on and cleared the end of the runway. It's kind of a short place to take off, but we made it." He broke ground at minimum takeoff speed and kept the aircraft low to build up climbing speed. When he had enough, he zoomed into the overcast.

The engine was purring well; neither it nor the propeller had been hit. Fisher decided to fly back to

Rescue at A Shau

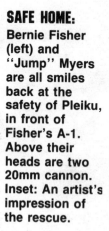

SAFE HOME:
Bernie Fisher (left) and "Jump" Myers are all smiles back at the safety of Pleiku, in front of Fisher's A-1. Above their heads are two 20mm cannon. Inset: An artist's impression of the rescue.

home base at Pleiku with his delighted and singed passenger. Myers was patched up and cleaned up, and rounded off his day with the news that he had been promoted to Lieutenant Colonel that morning.

By late afternoon the A Shau camp was lost. Sixteen US Marine H-34 helicopters were sent to bring out the survivors. Heavy enemy fire damaged the choppers, and destroyed two. Many choppers could not land. The civilian irregulars panicked. Of the original 277 defenders only 65 were evacuated. The few remaining men escaped on foot. Seven American Special Forces men, the two downed chopper crews, and ninety Vietnamese moved off in a northeasterly direction. A few were picked up by rescue aircraft in the next two days. The fate of the rest is not known.

Thuds go downtown

Target Hanoi, the toughest in the world

BY 1967, THE AIR defenses of North Vietnam were among the strongest in the world. Strategically important areas were well defended against the heaviest attacks, with a system of massed missiles and guns, along with radar and communications systems for controlling them.

To cope with the heavy defenses, the Air Force developed the "Wild Weasel" concept. At first, F-100F Super Sabres were used for these radar interference missions, but proved inadequate and too vulnerable. So the two-seat F-105F Thunderchief was fitted out for the missions. Manned by a pilot and an electronic warfare officer (nicknamed "bear"), the F-105F Wild Weasels carried a variety of radar warning and homing equipment, chaff to confuse radar, and radio jamming gear. They were armed with conventional bombs and cannon, plus air-to-ground missiles that rode down a radar beam to destroy its emitter.

The Wild Weasels flew in ahead of strike aircraft to confuse and jam the defenses, especially the SA-2 sites and their radars. They flew within range of enemy antiaircraft guns and SAMs to make their crews fire and expose their positions. They were armed bait, trolling in dangerous waters.

Captain Merlyn H. Dethlefsen flew a Wild Weasel F-105G from Takhli, Thailand. On 10 March 1967 a raid was launched against the Thai Nguyen steel works, about fifty miles north of Hanoi. Captain Dethlefsen and three other F-105 pilots had the job of knocking out the defenses around the mill.

The flight had the radio call sign Lincoln. Captain Dethlefsen and his "bear," Captain Kevin Gilroy, were Lincoln Three.

The Weasels topped up their tanks from KC-135

**F-105 Thud
Fairchild USAF
—The prototype
broke the sound
barrier on its
maiden flight,
22 October
1955. A single
jet was armed
with 20mm
cannon and
could carry a
bomb load up to
12,000 pounds.
The official
name was
Thunderchief,
but the Thud
nickname stuck.**

tankers on schedule, then crossed the Laos-North Vietnam border at medium altitude. Nearing the target, the lead Lincoln zoomed the flight to higher altitude, then rolled in to strike an active SAM site. Dethlefsen and his wingman, Major Kenneth Bell, were positioned a mile behind. The flak was so thick that the first two Thuds were completely obscured by the ugly black cloud of shell bursts. Number Two broke sharply to the right. Dethlefsen and his wingman followed.

The lead Lincoln had been hit hard. The two-man crew ejected in the flak. The beeper signals from their survival radios could be heard on the emergency channel. Number Two reported his own aircraft badly damaged and in trouble. Merl Dethlefsen took command of the mission.

He recalled, "The strike force was still vulnerable. We had fuel and missiles, guns and bombs, and the mission wasn't done yet." The lead Lincoln's missiles had missed the main SAM site. Dethlefsen decided to stay and carry out the mission. He maneuvered for his strike: "Coming around, I studied the flak pattern. It wasn't a matter of being able to avoid the flak, but of finding the least-intense areas." Major Bell, his wingman, commented: "When we got that kind of greeting at Thai Nguyen you know were were hitting something they wanted to hang on to."

On their first pass, Dethlefsen and Captain Gilroy were able to determine the location of the SAM site. Dethlefsen lined up for a second pass on the target when he spotted two MiG-21s closing in from his rear. He shot off a radar-seeking missile at the SAM site and dived away as one of the MiGs launched a missile at him. "I broke to the right, down through the flak. I figured that would give me the best chance of evading both the missile and MiGs' guns."

Standard procedure was for Thud pilots to avoid dogfights with the nimble interceptors, but Merl Dethlefsen decided to keep trying to knock out the defenses. Two more MiG-21s came at him. He evaded them by a sharp left break. But the laws of probability caught up with Lincoln Three, in the shape of a 57mm shell. It hit the fuselage and left wing, but the engine and flight controls continued to function.

Meanwhile the main strike force was blasting the

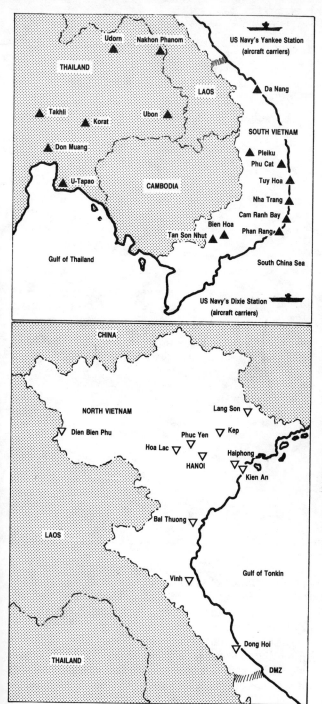

Thuds go downtown

THE BATTLEGROUND:
In South Vietnam and neighboring territories American forces assembled the largest array of aircraft ever to conduct the air war against the North. The enemy, by contrast, started the ten years of conflict without an air force but with a rapid influx of Soviet supplies was able to mount a defensive barrage of SAMs and antiaircraft fire that took its toll of US fliers.

Thuds go downtown

SAM CALL:
An SA-2 turns toward a photo reconnaissance aircraft above Phuc Yen MiG base, north of Hanoi. The SA-2 Guideline (inset) was 35 feet long and weighed more than 5,000 pounds. It could reach up to 60,000 feet and out to a range of 30 miles. A Soviet radar tracked the target, and steered the missile via a radio link. The 285-pound warhead had a proximity fuze; it did not have to achieve a direct hit to score a kill. Right: SA-2s on site, grouped around their radar truck. A favorite tactic was to surprise US pilots by launching through a cloud base.

Thai Nguyen mill with their bombs and missiles, raising clouds of smoke and dust that obscured the target and its defenses. Still Dethlefsen and his wingman remained over the target, even though Bell's aircraft had also been hit.

Dethlefsen had permission to stay after the main force left. He said: "I knew those fighter-bombers would be back tomorrow. With the weather the way it was that day, I knew we would never have a better chance. So I made up my mind to stay until I got

RADA

that SAM site or they got me."

While maneuvering around the flak he spotted another SAM site. He launched a radar-seeking missile and the site shut down. He dropped down to low level to see better, then used his radar direction-finding equipment to locate the original site. He found it, pulled up, and rolled in for a bombing pass. Ken Bell followed. Dethlefsen's CBU-24 fragmentation bombs blasted the site. He turned for another pass, raking it with his 20mm cannon. The site was

MIG-17: Subsonic, and never as deadly as the later MiG-21, the MiG-17 "Fresco" usually carried three 23mm cannon, and two racks of eight unguided 55mm air-to-air rockets. At low level the single seater was a highly maneuverable dogfighter, capable of tighter turns than heavier US jets.

engulfed in flames and explosions. Only then did Merlyn Dethlefsen pull up and head for an emergency forward base. The strikes he persisted in pressing repeatedly against what was called a wall of flak earned him a Medal of Honor, and made the raids on the Thai Nguyen complex achievable.

Six weeks later another Wild Weasel pilot was also to answer that call "far beyond duty." It came to Major Leo K. Thorsness of the 357th Tactical Fighter Squadron. Also based at Takhli, Thorsness was the most experienced hand in the 357th with nearly 100 missions. He was the man who instructed new crews.

On 19 April 1967, the target was the Xuan Mai barracks thirty miles southwest of Hanoi, where the Red River delta meets the hills. Leo Thorsness led a flight of four Thuds from Takhli. His backseat bear was Captain Harold E. Johnson.

The northeast monsoon still affected that part of the region. The weather over the target was turbulent, with broken cloud layers, poor visibility, and thunderstorms.

As the flight of Thuds flew toward the target, the distinctive rattlesnake tone in their headsets warned the men that the SA-2s' FAN SONG radars were being warmed up and were searching for them.

Major Thorsness sent two aircraft north of the target. He and his wingman flew to its south, heading toward the strongest SAM signals. He picked one, and launched a Shrike missile. The Shrike homed on the SAM's radar set, seven miles away. The signals from the SAM site ceased.

Thorsness spotted another SAM site and attacked it immediately. He and his wingman, Tom Madison, made a diving attack through a wall of 37mm and 57mm flak. They blew up the site with cluster bomb units. As they leveled off and accelerated, Tom Madison radioed that he was in trouble. He and his bear ejected. While that was happening, Leo Thorsness found a third SAM site, and launched a Shrike missile at its radar.

Thorsness shot down one MiG with his 20mm cannon as he circled over the descending parachutes of his wingmen, refueling twice to stay in the fight. They were finally captured after a Skyraider of the rescue force was shot down, and the rescue mission was abandoned.

Thorsness was not done. Another F-105 pilot radioed that he was lost and down to critical fuel. Thorsness and Johnson used their electronic gear to direct their own tanker to the lost pilot. He

SAM-KILLER:
An AGM-45 Shrike anti-radiation missile mounted on a Navy A-7E. With a range of 10 miles, the Shrike's homing head is turned on when the missile is still attached to the launch aircraft and is fired as soon as the seeker head locks onto a SAM. The enemy countered by developing an optical guidance system for the SA-2, so that missiles had no radar emissions to home on.

Master blaster —A 3,000-pound bomb slung under the wing of an F-105 at a base in Vietnam, December 1965. The early raids on targets like Thanh Hoa bridge showed that the standard 750-pounders lacked the power to damage a hard target. A typical load for a Thud going to war would be two 3,000-pounders and two external fuel tanks containing 1,100 gallons.

refueled just before his engine would have flamed out. By now Thorsness' Thud was critically low on fuel. He turned his F-105F toward the forward recovery base at Ubon, Thailand.

"We were indicating 'empty' when the runway came up in front of us, and we landed a little long. As we climbed out of the cockpit, Harry said something quaint like, 'That's a full day's work!'"

Eleven days later Leo Thorsness was shot down and captured in North Vietnam, where he was held prisoner for nearly six years. For that time the fact that he had been awarded the Medal of Honor was classified "secret-sensitive" so that he should not be singled out for ill treatment.

From May 1967, the bombing campaign against the North was stepped up, helped by exceptionally good weather. The focus was on rail lines and targets in the Hanoi and Haiphong areas (military targets in those former sanctuaries could now be struck).

A prime target now was the Paul Doumer bridge. Named after a 19th century governor general of French Indochina, it was at the junction of four of the five major rail lines. Destroying Paul Doumer would isolate Hanoi. The Joint Chiefs had wanted to strike the bridge in 1965. In August 1967 LBJ finally gave authorization.

More than 300 guns of 37, 57, 85, and 100mm caliber were sited around the bridge. They were reinforced in depth by 84 SA-2 sites plus MiG interceptors from Gia Lam, Phuc Yen, and Kep air bases.

The 7th Air Force made plans to strike "Downtown," as Hanoi was called. They had learned from the campaign against the Than Hoa bridge. The important lesson from that was the need to use heavy weapons. Thus the planners selected the F-105 Thud carrying 3,000-pound bombs.

The strike order came from Washington through CINCPAC in Hawaii and down to three fighter wings based in Thailand: the 355th Tactical Fighter Wing (TFW) at Takhli, the 388th TFW at Korat, and the 8th TFW at Ubon. The 355th TFW with its F-105 Thuds would lead the strike, carrying 3,000-pound bombs. The 388th TFW, also F-105s, and the 8th TFW, flying F-4s, would follow.

The strike message was decoded at 1100 on 11 August. Time over the target for the 355th was to be at 1558 hours. That meant takeoff time would be

Thunds go downtown

TRIPLE-A:
A 57mm antiaircraft cannon crew in action (above), and an eight-gun radar-controlled site near a bridge south of Hanoi (below). Soviet-designed air defense systems always had a strong layered element. The SA-2s were not effective until they achieved a minimum altitude of a few thousand feet. To outwit them, strike pilots tried flying below the SAMs' minimum altitude. As one report put it, "the cure was worse than the disease." The tactic dropped the strike aircraft right into the most lethal part of the antiaircraft gun envelope.

NIGHTHAWKS:
An F-105 being
fueled and
armed under
floodlights.
Pilots were
assigned
different
aircraft, but
each plane had
its own crew
chief who
regarded it as
strictly his
property.

at 1418 hours, with engines started at 1350 hours. Time was short. Worse still, the Thuds of the 355th were already loaded with the wrong ordnance—750-pound bombs. Weapons, fuel, and maintenance crews had been working through the night and early morning readying the aircraft for strikes against lesser targets. Now waiving normal safety rules, the wing's maintenance and weapons crews worked frantically to take off 750-pounders and hang 3,000-pound bombs on the twenty aircraft assigned to the mission.

Colonel John Giraudo was the wing commander. Mission commander to go Downtown this day was Colonel Bob White, the 355th's deputy commander for operations. They selected the most experienced

men in the wing to fly the mission. The crews gathered to be briefed. Briefing instructions on the target, tactics, and the likely opposition were in the planning package from 7th Air Force already on hand. The weather reports were perfect.

Up and down the busy flight line F-105s stood ready in the revetments. Heat waves shimmered off the concrete. The temperature was 93 degrees, but inside the revetments it seemed hotter. Briefings over, the pilots began the long preflight inspection of aircraft and armament. Then it was time to climb into cockpits overheated by the tropical midday sun.

The procedure begins. Put on the helmet. Groan at the heat, then proceed. Hook up oxygen mask to the aircraft system. Test by putting the mask to nose

Engine test —Clouds of smoke fill the air as a Thud ground crewman waits for the Pratt and Witney J-75 to ignite. With 25,000 pounds of thrust the reliable J-75 engines gave the F-105D its vital edge in combat—speed. Capable of flying over Mach 1 at ground level, and a theoretical maximum of Mach 2.2, the Thud always gave pilots the option of running fast from trouble.

and mouth, then breathe in while watching the half-moon indicator on the console. The mask is hung from the helmet on one side. Plug the communications jack into the socket. Check the cockpit to be sure that everything is where it should be.

The crew chief helps with the connections to the ejection seat, traces the shoulder harness to keep it straight, and the pilot hooks up his seat belt and shoulder harness.

Back to the final checklist. Sign the aircraft records for the crew chief. Start engines. One more Thud is now ready.

Then the aircraft taxis from revetments along taxiways, forming up in the assigned sequence. In the cockpits, the pilots close the Plexiglas canopies, check in with fellow flight members over the radio. Flight leaders check in with the mission commander. The first two F-105s take up position on the takeoff spot of Takhli's main runway. The pilots advance their throttles to bring the engines to takeoff power, holding the aircraft with the brakes.

On the dot at 1418 hours, the lead pilot released the brakes and began the takeoff roll. His wingman kept station at his side and slightly behind. As they rolled, the second pair in their flight taxied into position on the runway. Eleven seconds after the first pair started down the runway, the second pair began their takeoff. Eleven seconds after that, the third pair did the same. With the temperature in the mid-nineties and fully loaded, pairs of Thuds were taking approximately 29 seconds for takeoff.

The refuelling over Northern Laos went smoothly. The force crossed into North Vietnam. Four minutes from the target, the force was streaking along at about 600 knots and turning the northwest corner of Thud Ridge, the landmark pointing straight into Hanoi.

MiGs began taking off from Phuc Yen airfield, almost on their flight path, but the interceptors were not fast enough to turn and catch up with the F-105s.

The 355th TFW picked up the bridge clearly as they came off the southeast end of Thud Ridge. As planned, they swooped upward to 13,000 feet in echelon formation, rolling over to a 45-degree angle for the bomb run. As the first flight began its dive, a wall of flak started to reach up to it from the mass of antiaircraft guns below. The four-ship flak

suppression flight went to work. Their bombs completely obliterated a cluster of seven 85mm guns at the north side of the Red River. But other sites were still firing. No SAMs were observed launching.

The bomb run took only seven seconds. That was an eternity when the aircraft was diving straight toward a well-defended target at a 45-degree angle from 13,000 feet down to 8,000 feet. With the plane pointed at the target, the pilot released his bombs at 8,000 feet, deployed the F-105's speed brakes, pulled up, and made a hard turn to the left. Speed brakes were retracted, power added to afterburner, and the aircraft thundered over downtown Hanoi, heading to the east to re-form.

The 3,000-pound bombs from the first flight exploded squarely on target. The Number Two looked back and saw a bridge span splash into the water.

As the 355th strike force streaked east out of the area, the 8th TFW and 388th TFW forces followed. In the lead was a flight of four Wild Weasels, led by Lieutenant Colonel Jim McInerney.

The F-105G Wild Weasels of the 355th were kept close to the strike F-105s. McInerney's Weasels were employed differently. They ranged three to five

HOT SEAT:
A F-105 taxis out of the flightline at Da Nang, 1965. The white concrete reflected the midday tropical sun with blinding intensity while crew chiefs and pilots completed lengthy pre-flight routines. Only as they lined up for takeoff and the cockpit canopies were locked into place could the aircrafts' air conditioning systems work.

President Lyndon B. Johnson —He ordered the bombing halt of 1 November 1968, one of his last acts before leaving office.

minutes ahead of their strike force, looking for SAMs. When the bears picked up an active site, they attacked it.

McInerney saw no SAMs fired at the 355th attackers, but as the 388th force arrived, "all hell broke loose." His Weasels went to work against the SAM sites. McInerney and his "bear," Captain Fred Shannon, led their flight to destroy six SAM sites and damage four others. Both earned the Air Force Cross on this mission.

The strike knocked down two highway spans on the northeast side of the bridge. All told, 36 aircraft dropped 94 tons of bombs on the Paul Doumer bridge. The success of their mission stopped the movement of 26 trains per day, plus uncounted numbers of trucks.

Two aircraft were damaged by flak, but made it back to Thailand safely. No pilots were lost.

The North Vietnamese poured thousands of workers into recovering from the loss. They built a rail ferry a few miles downstream as a bypass, and began to reconstruct the dropped spans. On 24 August, Washington ordered that all targets in the Hanoi area were again restricted. Once again it was a sanctuary. Strikes could not be made against the rebuilding work.

By 3 October, less than two months after the first strike, the bridge was reopened for both rail and highway traffic.

The Hanoi area remained off-limits to strikes, until the prohibition was lifted on 23 October. On the 25th the monsoon lifted enough for 21 F-105s to press through and destroy two spans, a supporting pier, and part of the highway deck.

By 20 November the bridge was back in service. Bad weather prevented restrikes until mid-December.

There were no further strikes before President Johnson ordered a bombing halt that same month, in a further attempt to get Hanoi to the conference table. Strikes north of the 20th Parallel, and soon after that the 19th Parallel, were prohibited.

Then, on 1 November 1968, Johnson ordered a halt to all bombardment of North Vietnam. It would be more than four years before US strike aircraft would once again be able to strike strategic targets like the Paul Doumer bridge.

HANOI RR/HWY BR OV RED RIVER

1 DEC 67

BOMB IMP

REPAIRED SECTION

27 MAY 68

FLOATING CRANE

Thuds go downtown

DOUMER DOOMED: Recon photo shows bombs exploding around the Paul Doumer Bridge, Hanoi, while a raid is in progress in December 1967 (above). Repair work is going on five months later (below). The bridge comprised 19 steel spans. It was 5,532 feet long and 38 feet high. A rail track ran down the center, flanked on both sides by a ten-foot-wide highway. After the December raid, a ferry temporarily moved traffic, then in April a pontoon bridge opened four miles downstream. In all, 380 tons of ordnance were dropped on the bridge.

73

Bring 'em in close

Forward air controllers

IN MARCH 1965 US aircraft were authorized to strike wherever was necessary to support ground troops in South Vietnam. They were never to suffer the political restrictions that hampered air operations in the North.

Jets quickly arrived in South Vietnam with the primary mission of ground support. Marine F-4B Phantoms flew into Da Nang, and a brand-new Marine air base was constructed at Chu Lai, 57 miles down the coast. On 1 June, the first Marine A-4E Skyhawks from Marine Air Group 12 (MAG-12) flew in from the Philippines. Later, the potent F-4B Phantoms of VMFA-314, the "Black Knights," were based at Chu Lai.

Air Force wings equipped with the F-4C Phantom, then the most powerful and modern fighter in the world, were deployed to new bases in South Vietnam. In November 1965, the 12th Tactical Fighter wing arrived at Cam Ranh Bay and the 3d TFW arrived at Bien Hoa.

Also in 1965, B-52 strikes began in the South. Such was the power of these mighty strategic bombers, powered by eight jet engines, that at first General Westmoreland, the US commander in South Vietnam, used them only against known enemy targets away from cities and troop concentrations.

The first "Arc Light" mission, the saturation bombing of a square defined by a map grid, was flown by Strategic Air Command B-52s on 18 June against a base in War Zone D. The results were not encouraging: Two of the bombers collided during aerial refueling and were lost. Special Forces teams sent into the target area afterwards were driven off by sniper fire, suggesting that not much damage had been done. But the Arc Light strikes became so

In control —Airmen plot positions on a Plexiglas screen at the Direct Air Support Center at Binh Thuy air base, South Vietnam. For nonemergency missions, air liaison officers forwarded requests for air support in advance, along with target details, location of friendly troops, and suggested ordnance, to the DASC, which allocated aircraft available. Frequently they had to rethink their plans with little notice when a priority call came in.

consistently accurate that in November 1965 the first B-52 strikes in direct support of ground troops were flown.

Troops of the 1st Cavalry Division were in a fierce fight with two North Vietnamese Army (NVA) regiments in the Ia Drang valley. It was the first major foray into the South by North Vietnamese regulars.

The NVA and accompanying VC units were about to overwhelm the friendlies, until on 16 November a force of eighteen B-52s was thrown together and dispatched to drop 344 tons of bombs on enemy positions. After fierce fighting by the Cav, helped by 96 Arc Light sorties and 300 by tactical strike aircraft such as F-4s and F-100s, the NVA were beaten back.

The essential element for coordinating air support for ground units was the air liaison officer (ALO). Air liaison officers were USAF fighter pilots assigned to duty with Army combat units. They functioned as the primary advisers to the ground commanders on air operation matters. When the bullets were flying, however, the men who mattered were the forward air controllers (FACs), the flying link between forces on the ground and strike aircraft. ALOs also flew as FACs.

All ground combat units were able to call upon an FAC when needed. He usually flew in the same area, and quite often for the same ground units. His were often the first eyes to spot changes that developed into useful intelligence information. When he found the enemy, he would request approval to call in air strikes. Or if an air strike against a known enemy target had been preplanned, the FAC would be on hand to mark it for the strike aircraft.

FACs were fighter pilots who had also been trained in air-ground operations, had gone to jungle survival school, and had learned the basics of ground combat operations. Their knowledge of fighter tactics helped in controlling air strikes. Their familiar voices on the radio when talking with ground units gave confidence to the troops.

When an operation was under way, or troops engaged the enemy, the FAC was a very busy man flying very low in a very small and slow airplane. To the enemy he was an easy target, but they were often reluctant to fire on an FAC, for fear of attracting attention. On the occasions when they were not

Bring 'em in close

HEADS DOWN:
A Marine F-4B Phantom releases a 500-pound Snakeye bomb. Fins at the base of the bomb opened to slow its fall through the air, allowing the aircraft time to escape from the blast zone with no danger of damage. A combination of these "retarded" bombs and napalm—"Snake and Nape"—was one of the deadliest close-support weapons loads because of the accuracy of their low-level delivery and the combined effect of blast and flame.

Bring 'em in close

CLOSE UP: An FAC in the air. Note the white phosphorous marking rockets in tubes on each wing. The FAC was wedged into the front seat along with survival kit, an armored vest, an M-16 rifle, a .38-cal pistol, a knife, and a bag of smoke grenades. Maps and communications codes for the day were strapped on his legs. He had several different colored pencils to mark the maps and make notes. His navigation was by pilotage: looking out the window and using his map.

reluctant to bring him down, the FAC relied on his flying skill to evade fire. As he maneuvered he would operate his three main radios, talking on VHF and UHF to strike aircraft, and on the FM net used by the ground commanders.

In his cramped cockpit, the FAC baked in the sun. The first FACs flew 0-1 Birddogs with side windows that opened to let in a breeze. (They also chucked smoke grenades out of them when marking enemy positions on the ground.)

Captain Hilliard A. Wilbanks was an FAC flying in support of the South Vietnamese 23d Ranger Battalion on 24 February 1967. The Rangers, with American advisers, were searching for a Viet Cong unit near Di Linh. Earlier in the day, the VC had ambushed and decimated another South Vietnamese unit, killing its American advisers and capturing their radios.

At dusk, the 23d Rangers moved slowly through the low bushes of a tea plantation in the hills.

Cooperation —A forward air controller and the commander of an Army Special Forces camp at Plei Djereng, in the highlands of South Vietnam, conferring before a day's operations. The Special Forces credited the FACs' ability to summon firepower with keeping the border outposts from being overrun.

Nearby, two US Army helicopter gunships hovered, ready to deliver fire support when needed.

Captain Wilbanks ranged overhead in his Birddog. This was his 488th mission in ten months. He had just two months of his one-year tour left. As he flew, searching the area, he talked on the radio to the senior American adviser with the Rangers and to the gunships.

Suddenly, from his aerial vantage point, Wilbanks saw the enemy ambush ahead. He called a warning to the Rangers. As the Rangers reacted to his message, the enemy sprang the ambush with heavy fire from mortars, small arms, machine guns, and automatic rifles. Two Ranger companies were pinned down immediately, with heavy casualties in the forward units.

Captain Wilbanks banked, aimed his aircraft, and fired a white phosphorous rocket into the center of the enemy position. The white smoke identified it as a target for the helicopter gunships. They swung into action, hosing down the enemy with rockets and machine guns. But an enemy .50-caliber machine gun damaged one of the helicopters badly. Captain Wilbanks advised the undamaged gunships to escort the damaged one out of the fray.

Over the radio another FAC relayed the information that two flights of fighters were on their way.

But then Wilbanks saw the Viet Cong rising from their ambush holes. He realized the fighters would be too late. The VC were starting to charge down the slope toward the Rangers, who were pinned down and already badly mauled. The gunships were gone and the fighters were still on the way.

Wilbanks rolled his O-1 Birddog like a fighter and slammed a white phosphorous (WP) rocket into the middle of the VC line. They stopped their charge and turned their guns on him. Wilbanks rolled the Birddog and turned again, slamming another WP rocket into their ranks. He was now a strike aircraft. The VC fire became intense, as they concentrated on his small darting craft. He jinked and weaved, then straightened out to fire a fourth rocket into the enemy.

It was his last one, and everyone knew it. By rights he should have turned off the target and waited for the fighters to arrive. No one would have criticized that. He had already delayed the enemy assault with

Bring 'em in close

EYES IN THE SKY:
An FAC in his
0-1 Birddog
above a
smouldering
patch of forest
after a napalm
strike on a Viet
Cong camp near
Pleiku, Central
Highlands.
Flying at low
level, the FAC
could spot the
telltale signs of
enemy activity
and accurately
direct fire, but
his fragile
plane's lack of
protection was a
considerable
liability.

his rockets. But Wilbanks still had unexpected firepower to use to protect the Rangers—his M-16 automatic rifle.

He rolled in again, pointing his Birddog toward the enemy. Releasing the controls, he leaned out of the aircraft to fire the rifle from the right-hand side window. His amazing action temporarily baffled the enemy. He grabbed the controls, swung above the scene, and reloaded another magazine of ammunition. The American advisers with the Rangers were

Bring 'em in close

FIERY TRAIL: An F-100 Supersabre looses a pod full of rockets at a VC position in thick jungle. The "Hun" became the workhorse of close air support operations, where its short range and relatively light bomb load (roughly half that of the F-105) were not too great a disadvantage. Jets—"fast-movers"—were used for close support where conditions allowed, in daylight with good visibility, because they were much harder for the VC gunners to hit.

as amazed as the VC when Wilbanks made another rifle-firing pass, spraying automatic fire into the enemy. Captain R. J. Wooten, the senior adviser, told how Wilbanks's plane was so close they could hear it being hit by the enemy bullets.

Even though hit, Wilbanks turned his aircraft, reloaded his rifle, and bored in for a third rifle pass. Captain Gary Vote, another adviser with the Rangers, said, "He was no more than 100 feet off the ground, firing his rifle. Then he began the erratic

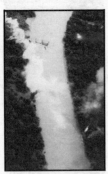

Pilot's view —Smoke and flames boil over a Viet Cong riverside warehouse in the Mekong Delta as an F-100 fires 2.75-inch rockets in a diving attack. In this attack Supersabres of the 481st Tactical Fighter Squadron destroyed 11 VC buildings and 3 sampans.

moves. I thought he was wounded and looking for a friendly spot to land. I jumped up and waved my arms. But as he banked again, I could see that he was unconscious. His aircraft crashed about 100 meters away."

The Birddog hit between the two forces. Captain Vote got to it, and pulled Captain Wilbanks from the wreckage. He was still alive.

Two gunships returned, firing into the enemy and trying to land to rescue Wilbanks. But the heavy fire drove them off after four attempts. Another FAC had arrived. He directed the 20mm cannon fire of two F-4 Phantoms into the enemy while a helicopter braved the fire to lift out Captain Wilbanks. He died in the helicopter en route to medical treatment. Captain Hilliard A. Wilbanks was awarded the Medal of Honor for his gallantry and sacrifice of his life for others.

UNITS IN CONTACT with the enemy had priority during air strikes. This is how a dialogue over the air waves might have gone after an infantry platoon had run into a major ambush by North Vietnamese regulars. The request for air support is passed first to the forward air controller, from him to the air liaison officer, and from him to the direct air support center (DASC), which had the task of coordinating all the strikes in the area. The radio conversations might sound like this:

INFANTRY COMMANDER *(on FM)* to FAC: Helix One-Two (the FAC's call sign), this is Boxer Six. We need an air strike right now!
FAC in Birddog over the action *(on FM)*: Roger, Boxer Six. We'll get one for you.
FAC *(Switches to UHF, calls ALO)*: Helix One-One, this is Helix One-Two. Request immediate for Boxer. Troops in contact, estimated NVA company in bunkers, automatic weapons and rocket launchers.
ALO in command helicopter *(on UHF)*: Roger, on the way.

The ALO calls the DASC on UHF. He reports the situation—troops in contact—and requests an immediate air strike. The ALO also requests another strike to follow in fifteen minutes. This lets the

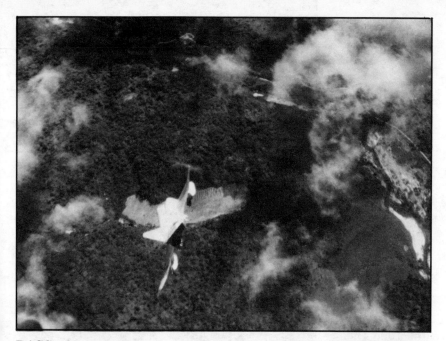

DASC take two actions: divert a flight in the air that will reach the scene in five minutes or so, and launch a standby alert flight. If the situation is really desperate, the DASC can divert all strike flights in the region, funneling them into the FAC's control.

Fighters arrive over the scene.

> STRIKE FIGHTER LEAD *(on UHF)*: Hello, Helix One-Two. Silver Four-One here. Flight of four F-4Cs, sixteen Mark 82s (500-pound general purpose bombs), eight napes (napalm), and plenty 20 mike-mike (the 20mm Gatling cannon).

ALO monitors the fighter's transmission on his UHF set, informs the brigade commander. Brigade commander passes the welcome word to the ground troops on his own FM command net. This keeps useless chatter off the FM frequency between the FAC and the troops in contact.

> FAC *(on UHF)*: Silver Four-One, this is Helix One-Two. Glad to have you. We have a company in contact with NVA. An estimated company in bunkers along a tree line. Troops

PHANTOM STRIKE:
In the classic fighter-bomber's maneuver, an Air Force pilot rolls his F-4C over so that he can keep his target (off picture, bottom left) in view all the way down to weapons release. As close support, as a long-range bomber, or as a dogfighter, the Phantom II was the outstanding weapons system of the Vietnam War.

Bring 'em in close

THANKS, GUYS: Blackhorse troopers of the 11th Armored Cavalry sent this picture to the 3d Tactical Fighter Wing at Bien Hoa as a way of saying thanks for the air support they received during the Toan Thang offensive, 1968. It shows bomb blasts on an enemy trench system northwest of Saigon, and demonstrates how close air strikes could be called when friendly troops have armored protection.

will pop smoke. I'll mark the target. Friendlies are on line northeast to southwest. Recommend your passes be parallel. Mark 82s on first pass. Stand by.

(FAC switches to FM radio.)

FAC *(on FM)*: Boxer Six, Helix One-Two. Four fighters ready to drop bombs, then napalm, then strafe. Pop smoke when ready.

INFANTRY *(on FM)*: Roger, popping smoke.

The infantry throw out a colored smoke grenade. It roils and billows upward.

FAC *(on FM)*: I have green smoke.

The FAC is required to call out the smoke. If the infantry called the color first and the enemy was listening, they could—and did—throw out the same color, confusing the FAC and the fighters.

    INFANTRY *(on FM)*: Green is correct. Bring 'em in close!

Meanwhile, the fight on the ground continues. Friendly mortars and artillery are crumping on the enemy positions. The brigade's artillery commander and ALO consult in the command helicopter. The mortar and artillery fires are shifted to clear a path for the strike aircraft, but not stopped or lifted.

> FAC (on FM): On the way.
> FAC (switches to UHF): Silver Four-One, friendlies at green smoke. Marking target now. Target is 100 meters from green smoke on a heading of 300 degrees.

FAC rolls his Birddog into position to fire a 2.75-inch white phosphorous marking rocket. He is most vulnerable at this moment. His rocket must hit precisely on the enemy position, so he must be close and low.

> FAC (on UHF): This is Helix One-Two. Put your first Mark 82s on my smoke.
> FIGHTER LEAD (on UHF): We have the green smoke. We have your smoke. Lead is hot and in.

The Phantoms have been barely visible until now, cruising high in the hot sky. A dirty smoke trail, a Phantom trademark, is the most visible sign. Now the lead aircraft rolls from his perch and streaks earthward at a 45-degree angle, the sun reflecting off his canopy. The lead Phantom grows in size; the rumble of its two J-79 jet engines swells to a screeching roar. The FAC is jinking his O-1 about the air, keeping his smoke marker and the enemy in sight, at the same time avoiding friendly artillery and the jet's bomb run.

Two black ovals detach themselves from the diving Phantom. The 500-pound bombs are headed for the enemy positions. The Phantom pilot pulls up and zooms skyward. The roar of his engines seems loud until the bombs explode. Then two blasts rend the air, dirt and smoke fly, and two gray clouds rise close together, marking the impact point. The air is still vibrating with the blast when the radios crackle into life again.

> INFANTRY (on FM): Got 'em! Good shot. Now hit them about twenty meters north, Helix One-Two.

The watchers —A machine gun squad of M company, 7th Marines, studies the treeline as an air strike goes in. The object was to see if any Viet Cong were driven into the open by the blast, which probably fell a few yards too far into the woodlot to have the desired effect.

FAC *(on FM)*: Roger that (switching to UHF). Silver Four-One, right on target. The crunchies liked that one. Silver Four-Two, put your Mark 82s about twenty meters to the north. If you hit inside the edge of the smoke cloud, you'll be fine.

FIGHTER NO. 2 *(on UHF)*: Silver Four-Two. Wilco. Two is hot and in.

The second Phantom pilot rolls his aircraft over and begins his attack.

INFANTRY *(on FM)*: That was wide, Helix. Too far north. Nobody there. Bring it in closer.

FAC *(on FM)*: Right, will do.

FAC *(on UHF)*: Silver Four-Two, that was a bit wide by about fifty meters. Silver Four-Three, put your bombs between the first two and we've got a winner.

FIGHTER NO. 3 *(on UHF)*: Silver Four-Three, wilco, hot and rolling in.

TEAM SPIRIT: The men who made flight missions possible, from pilot and observer to fireman (in silver flameproof suit), pose with their latest arrival, an OV-10A Bronco, at the Marine air base at Marble Mountain, near Da Nang, 1968.

Falling like water

WHILE AIR support was available rapidly and effectively for thousands of firefights in South Vietnam, often at just a few minutes' notice, there can have been few battles in history where it has been so deliberately and precisely employed as in the defense of Khe Sanh.

The Marines' base at Khe Sanh was critically located in Quang Tri Province, nine kilometers from the border with Laos. It sat on the old Route Nationale 9 that led by the shortest route from Laos across the narrow northern neck of Vietnam to Quang Tri. An enemy wanting to infiltrate men and supplies into South Vietnam, or to cut off a chunk of the country, would have to pass the Khe Sanh area.

In early January 1968, the increasing tempo of enemy attacks in the area seemed to indicate to General Westmoreland that North Vietnam's General Vo Nguyen Giap was planning an all-out attempt to take the base, then manned by a battalion of the 26th Marines—eventually to be reinforced to three times that number.

Westmoreland did not have enough troops to destroy the enemy forces. He had two alternatives at Khe Sanh: dig in and hold, or pull out. If he withdrew the Marines, the enemy would have Khe Sanh by default, gaining control of an important part of the country and also achieving an important psychological victory.

President Johnson himself took a personal interest in what was clearly destined to be a momentous battle. He demanded assurances from the Joint Chiefs of Staff downward that the position could and should be held. In the back of everybody's mind was Giap's crucial victory 14 years earlier against the French

Falling like water

BOMB CARRIER:
A cutaway diagram of a six-crew B-52D. It carried eighty-four 500- or 750-pound bombs on underwing pylons and in the internal bomb bay. Precision high-altitude bombing was achieved using Combat Skyspot, a radar bombing control system developed from a computerized scorer for dummy attacks on exercises. Factors such as altitude, wind speed and direction, aircraft speed, temperature, and bomb characteristics were processed to produce the heading, altitude, and airspeed the plane should maintain.

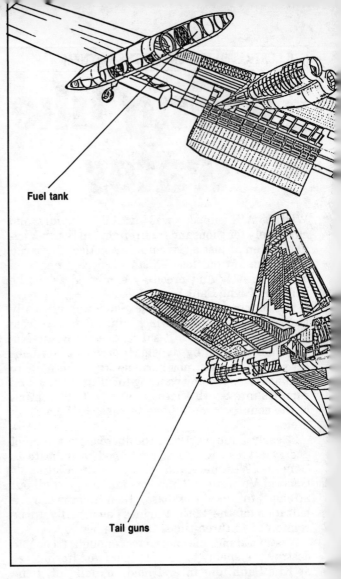

Fuel tank

Tail guns

at another distant, fog-shrouded outpost: Dien Bien Phu.

Johnson got his assurances: Khe Sanh would hold. If they really wanted it, the NVA would have to come and get it.

Westmoreland based his defense plans on air power from the outset. In the autumn of 1967 a Marine camp at Con Thien had been saved by a savage air bombardment of the attackers, combined with an aggressive mobile defense. Here was an

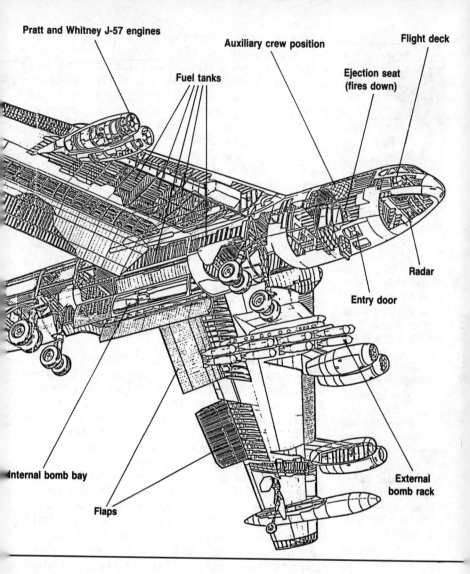

Pratt and Whitney J-57 engines

Auxiliary crew position

Flight deck

Fuel tanks

Ejection seat
(fires down)

Radar

Entry door

Internal bomb bay

External
bomb rack

Flaps

opportunity to repeat the exercise, although the
defenders at Khe Sanh were to remain locked inside
the perimeter.

He called the operation Niagara. "I visualized
your bombs falling like water over the famous falls
there in northern New York State," he was later to
tell the 3d Air Division at Guam. But first there was
Niagara I, a meticulous and extensive reconnaissance operation combining the latest photo-
graphic and electronic techniques with good old-

Bombing up —Ground crewmen loading 750-pound bombs onto a B-52 at Guam, 2,000 miles from Khe Sanh. The bombs were shipped in sections and assembled on the base by munitions maintenance teams. At the time this picture was taken, in August 1965, bombs were still loaded on racks one by one. Later, the racks would be pre-loaded away from the aircraft. A typical B-52 base would shift 21,000 bombs in a week.

fashioned scouting over the hills of Quang Tri. The garrison was ordered to dig in deep. Outposts on the surrounding key terrain were reinforced and also dug in. Highway 9, the road from the coastal bases to Khe Sanh, was unusable. Resupply and medical evacuation were entirely by air. The monsoon was at its wettest, with rain, mist, and low ceilings.

On January 14, General Westmoreland ordered the strike phase of Operation Niagara to begin. The big B-52s of 3d Air Division began dropping tons of high explosive on enemy storage, staging, and assembly areas. At first they could drop no closer to friendly positions than 3,000 meters. Marine, Navy, and Air Force fighter-bombers struck enemy positions closer in. Heavy artillery began around-the-clock shelling of the enemy positions.

Undeterred by a week's bombardment, NVA troops attacked and overran Khe Sanh village. The troop perimeter contracted around the combat base's airfield. Westmoreland reinforced the base with another battalion of Marines and an ARVN Ranger battalion.

The siege was on. Two NVA divisions, with an estimated 20,000 to 30,000 troops, were committed to it. They overran the nearby Lang Vei Special Forces camp on 6 February, removing a key listening post. Their artillery was emplaced on high ground overlooking the airfield. The NVA howitzers fired continuously, being easily resupplied from their large storage area only a few kilometers west in Laos.

The siege of Khe Sanh is an epic story. The Marines held their ground against eleven weeks of unremitting siege and bombardment by the best the NVA could field. On one day, 23 February, a total of 1,307 enemy mortar, rocket, and artillery rounds fell on the base. The Marines held on through sheer determination and valiant and skillful application of air striking power and airlift.

The B-52s flew 2,602 sorties from mid-January to the end of March, dropping more than 75,000 tons of bombs through the monsoon overcast day and night. By almost superhuman maintenance and servicing efforts, 3d Air Division was able to keep an unbroken stream of B-52s coming over Khe Sanh: six aircraft every three hours.

The bombers were directed by radar and computers using a system called Combat Skyspot, which could precisely calculate the bomb release spot for each cell of three B-52s to accurately blanket a one-kilometer by two-kilometer box through the thickest cloud.

Forward air controllers over the base simultaneously coordinated attacks by lighter aircraft. The onslaught was massive. At times flights of jet fighters were stacked like airliners over Chicago's O'Hare, in a holding pattern extending as high as 35,000 feet, gradually descending as plane after plane dropped its bombs.

On 30 January, the enemy's Tet Offensive broke over the cities of South Vietnam. Air strikes by fighter-bombers and B-52s were essential elements of the fight to overcome the attacks. The monthly B-52 sortie rate leaped upward from 800 in 1967 to 1,200 in early February and to 1,800 by mid-February. Fortunately the 3d Air Division's 94 aircraft were reinforced with 26 more by February 7, flying from Kadena AFB, Okinawa.

The siege continued. Enemy attacks were smashed before they started by split-second coordination of B-52 and tactical air strikes, long-range artillery, and 105mm and mortar fire from inside the camp to create barriers of fire. By March B-52 strikes were regularly called as close as one kilometer to friendly troops.

In early April 1968, the monsoon broke and good weather returned. The 1st Air Cavalry Division attacked from the coast to relieve Khe Sanh, leapfrogging to key hilltops to command the rebuilding of the road and destruction of the remaining enemy. When the Cav was close enough, the Khe Sanh garrison attacked eastward to link up.

The siege of Khe Sanh ended on 15 April 1968.

There was no question that air power could take credit for a massive victory, but it was hard to assess how much damage the bombers had caused, so often had the ground been blasted.

The most accurate assessments were made by Marine patrols. A B-52 raid on March 19 left a mess of craters on top of craters that defied the most skilled photo interpreters, but a patrol later found that a bunker complex big enough to have contained a battalion (roughly 1,000 men) had been destroyed.

Captured diaries and letters from NVA soldiers

Inside the wire —A Marine officer watches the results of a Phantom strike close to the Khe Sanh perimeter. FACs coordinated artillery and tactical aircraft to deal with threats close to the wire, using the B-52s to smash concentrations further out. This F-4 has bombed at a shallow angle, for maximum accuracy.

Falling like water

KILLING GROUND: Bombs dropped by B-52s land on a VC staging area. A single strike is said to have killed more than 1,000 men—three quarters of a regiment. The Stratofortresses flew so high they could neither be seen nor heard in the target area. The lack of any warning of an attack before the bombs started to explode could produce devastating psychological effects even among those in the target area who escaped physically unharmed.

also gave clues to the effect of air strikes on enemy morale. One document contained a note that Khe Sanh was a fiercer battle than Dien Bien Phu because the unceasing pounding by the B-52s killed even those hiding in caves or underground. A notebook said 300 men had deserted from one unit, size unknown, because of the intensity of the air raids.

General Westmoreland reported, "the key to our success at Khe Sanh was firepower, principally aerial firepower. Between 22 January and 31 March, tactical aircraft flew an average of 300 sorties daily,

close to one every five minutes, and expended 35,000 tons of bombs and rockets.

"At the same time, increasing numbers of the Strategic Air Command's B-52s were demonstrating their devastating ability to neutralize a large area. The B-52s flew 2,602 sorties and dropped over 75,000 tons of bombs during the siege and were instrumental in preventing the enemy from assembling in large formations."

Westmoreland told 3d Air Division, in a speech on 13 June 1968: "The thing that broke their backs was basically the fire of the B-52s."

Night gunships

Covering the US withdrawal

IN 1967 THE Vietnamese Air Force began to move into the jet age, receiving a squadron of Northrop F-5 Freedom Fighter interceptors. By mid-1969 three more squadrons had converted to Cessna A-37 Dragonfly light strike aircraft. These two types of aircraft were capable of defensive missions. But their limited combat range under 200 nautical miles made them unsuitable for offensive operations. Deliveries speeded up under the "Vietnamization" program, which started in 1969 with the objective of turning the defense of South Vietnam over to the Vietnamese themselves and progressively withdrawing American forces.

In South Vietnam, the withdrawal of US troops and increase in ARVN forces changed the role of US strike aircraft. With Vietnamization taking hold in 1969–1971, the VNAF increased its sorties. US air power's role became less involved in day strikes supporting troops in contact with the enemy. More US flights were flown in aid of bases and villages under attack. There was an increase in night missions, which created a problem solved by the use of gunships like the AC-47 Spooky, invented years earlier.

At night FACs could be of little use flying above a firefight. And fast jets found it hard even to find a target marked by flickering flares. Nighttime had become the enemy's favorite time for attacks, largely because of the protection the darkness offered against air strikes. The problem was an urgent one. Experimentation resulted in some of the most remarkable aircraft to fly over Vietnam, transports modified with elaborate sensors and illumination devices, carrying awesome firepower.

The first examples were the AC-47 gunships, at

Commando hunt area

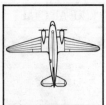

AC-47 Spooky Douglas USAF —The Gooney Bird transport of the 1930s and 1940s was modified in the 1960s as a powerful gunship. Spooky carried three 7.62mm miniguns, each capable of firing 6,000 rounds per minute, plus up to 56 flares for long illumination of targets at night. Spooky's accurate stream of gunfire and bright illumination were credited with saving innumerable positions under night attack by enemy forces.

first nicknamed "Puff the Magic Dragon." They were rugged old C-47 transports converted into fearsome deliverers of streams of firepower from their side-firing minigun pods. The miniguns were rapid-fire 7.62mm Gatling-type guns developed by General Electric. Their multiple barrels spewed up to 6,000 rounds per minute in a very accurate cone of fire.

The AC-47 performed well. But its payload was relatively small and its engines did not have the power needed in the mountainous highlands. Gradually the need for more modern aircraft became apparent. Two other transport aircraft, the Fairchild C-119 Flying Boxcar and the Lockheed C-130 Hercules, were modified as gunships. In addition to larger payloads, both were high-wing aircraft, better suited for side-firing weapons than the low-wing C-47.

The AC-130s, nicknamed "Spectre," joined the AC-47s and other strike aircraft in Operation Commando Hunt, interdicting the Ho Chi Minh Trail in southern Laos. The gunships turned out to be the most efficient truck-killers. They were equipped for night operations, flew slower, and had newer sensors, capable of detecting movement on the ground.

A typical gunship mission was that of 14th Air Commando Wing's Spectre 01, an AC-130 based at Ubon, Thailand, on the night of 30 December 1968, the first to have a preplanned fighter escort for flak suppression.

Within ten minutes of takeoff the gunship was crossing the fence into Laos and making radio contact with Moonbeam, the ABCCC (airborne command control center) operating over southern Laos. Using current intelligence, Moonbeam assigned Spectre 01 an operating area.

According to the mission report: "At 1840 hours, four eastbound 'movers' were detected. The sensor inputs fed the fire-control computer, and the information reflected in the pilot's gunsight as he turned into a left orbit at 4,500 feet AGL (above ground level). Selecting the lead truck to stall traffic, the pilot pushed the trigger button as the movable and fixed target reticles superimposed in his gunsight. The 1,000 rounds of 20mm, fired in a four-minute attack, damaged one truck.

"At 1855, Spectre 01 detected Target 2—one mover—and in a two-minute attack orbit fired another 1,000 rounds of 20mm, damaging one truck. Farther down the road the gunship discovered three stationary trucks and a suspected truck park. While marking the area with flares, Spectre 01 met with 37mm AAA (antiaircraft) fire. From 1902 to 1925 hours, the pilot squeezed off 1,000 more rounds of 20mm on both the suspected truck park and the 37mm site. An explosion and fire told of the AAA emplacement's destruction.

"Two more stationary trucks became Target 4. Spectre 01 attacked from 2002 to 2006 hours and damaged both of them. Two F-4 flights—call signs Schlitz and Combine—worked on AAA sites together with Spectre strikes and claimed two sites destroyed. From 2021 to 2026 hours, Spectre 01 once more fired 1,000 20mm rounds upon return to the scene of the suspected truck park of Target 3. No visual results were obtained of this final attack. Spectre 01 left the target area at 2035 hours after an elapsed time of 3 hours and 15 minutes, with 6,000 rounds of 20mm and fifteen MK-6 flares expended.

"The night's work totaled four trucks damaged, one 37mm antiaircraft site destroyed, and one 37mm AAA site silenced. Spectre 01 recrossed the fence and touched down at Ubon at 2115 hours. Total mission time stood at four hours and ten minutes."

Early in 1970, the numbers of Commando Hunt sorties tailed off, hit by cost restrictions and higher priorities given to missions in other places. These included northern Laos, where the Communist Pathet Lao had become more active, and Cambodia, which was invaded by US and Vietnamese forces in May 1970, with heavy support from the air, to try to counter growing Communist incursions.

North Vietnam continued to push men and munitions down the trail network, and to rebuild its forces for another assault into South Vietnam when the time was right. Late in 1970, it looked to Allied intelligence analysts as if the NVA was preparing to launch an offensive in I Corps, the northernmost provinces of South Vietnam. Supplies began to accumulate in huge stockpiles at the hub town of Tchepone in central Laos.

General Creighton Abrams, now the commander of US forces in Vietnam (CINCMACV), and Ambassador Ellsworth Bunker proposed an operation to cut westward from the Khe Sanh area, take

Big gun —The AC-130's 105mm had a special recoil system so that the aircraft was not shaken to bits by the blast. The 105mm was the only weapon carried that could stop tanks. Near it was one of the 40mm guns and a 2-kilowatt searchlight, which could operate in either visible or infra-red modes. Mounting all the weapons on the same side was the only effective design for a gunship, but once a Spectre began rotating around a target it provided a totally predictable flight path for enemy gunners.

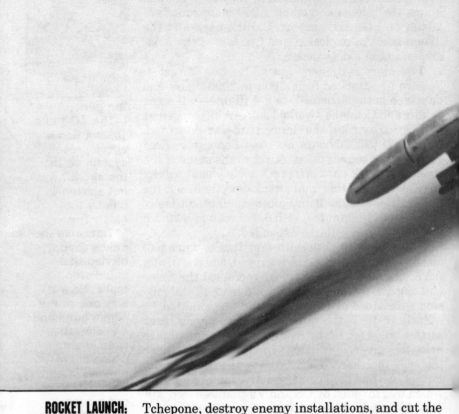

ROCKET LAUNCH:
An A-37 unloads a pod of rockets on a target in South Vietnam. The Dragonfly had poor performance compared to most front-line aircraft in Vietnam, but was an effective light ground support platform.

Tchepone, destroy enemy installations, and cut the Ho Chi Minh Trail.

The operation would be called Lam Son 719. Congressional restrictions prohibited the use of US ground troops outside of South Vietnam, so ARVN forces would perform the actual invasion of Laos. US ground units would secure leap-off points such as Khe Sanh, and US air power would support the ARVN forces. This was a big gamble, but if it worked, the results would be worth the risk. If Lam Son 719 were successful, enemy potential for a major thrust into South Vietnam could be damaged severely; the enemy would have to wait for more than a year, until the dry season of October 1972 through May 1973, to strike at the heart of South

Vietnam. Most of the heavy striking power had to come from USAF, Navy, and Marine aircraft. They were controlled by US forward air controllers (FACs). But they lacked an American ground link. US advisers were not allowed to accompany the ARVN ground units into action.

The FACs had a language problem partly solved by installing English-speaking Vietnamese in the FAC and other control aircraft. That patchwork solution slowed down reaction time and often led to misunderstanding.

Notwithstanding the complexities, Lam Son 719 pushed off on 8 February 1971, with 6,200 ARVN troops airlifted to selected locations inside Laos. They built fire support bases and patrolled from

John Levitow
—The giant
magnesium
flares used by
the AC-47
gunships were a
hazard to the
aircraft carrying
them. In
February 1969,
Airman 1st
Class John L.
Levitow earned
the Medal of
Honor when he
threw himself
on top of a flare
that had been
triggered by an
enemy shell and
was about to
ignite in the rear
compartment of
his gunship.
Despite being
seriously
wounded, he
managed to
drag the flare to
the aircraft's
rear door and
jettison it a
fraction of a
second before it
exploded.
Levitow
returned to duty
in Vietnam after
recovering.

them. The ARVN actions were protected by heavy B-52 and tactical air strikes on NVA positions and lines of communication. The aircraft carrier USS *Hancock* steamed closer to the coast to support the operation. Navy A-4Fs from attack squadrons VA-55 and VA-164 aboard the carrier joined Air Force F-4 and F-100 aircraft in tactical strikes. At night, AC-130 Specter and AC-119K Stinger gunships covered the ARVN units.

Four days after the invasion began, ARVN troop strength in Laos reached 17,000. They pushed deliberately westward toward Tchepone against light resistance. But the weather did not go according to plan, with the rains falling earlier than normal. That made for a muddy main road (Highway 9) and hampered the use of air power.

Otherwise the invasion continued to plan until 25 February, when the North Vietnamese launched a surprise counteroffensive with more than 35,000 troops, twice the ARVN strength. For the first time, the NVA used armor in force, deploying more than 120 Soviet-built tanks and large numbers of AAA guns. The AAA inflicted heavy losses on low-flying US Army helicopters.

The ARVN units held, largely thanks to American airpower. MACV (Military Assistance Command Vietnam) headquarters in Saigon estimated that the B-52 strikes alone were killing the equivalent of one NVA regiment per week. ARVN units resumed their westward advance on 3 March. A week later enemy reinforcements began to menace the advance units at Tchepone and the long supply line stretching back to Khe Sanh. The ARVN commander, Lieutenant General Hoang Xuan Lam, decided to cut the operation short, and ordered a withdrawal that soon turned into a hasty retreat.

During Lam Son 719, both sides suffered heavy casualties. NVA dead were estimated at 14,500. Air strikes destroyed 1,530 trucks and 74 tanks, plus thousands of tons of fuel and ammunition. ARVN forces suffered 1,519 killed and lost 75 tanks. US losses were more than 100 Army helicopters and 7 fighter-bombers.

On the positive side, Lam Son 719 forced Hanoi to delay its major offensive against the South for another year. It also bought time for Washington and Saigon to speed the pace of Vietnamization and

withdrawal of US forces. Only two US Navy carriers remained on station in the Gulf of Tonkin as 1972 began, and the number of Air Force strike aircraft based in Vietnam had dropped to less than 90 by early 1972.

In Thailand, only 225 strike aircraft were left. Several USAF tactical fighter wings were either inactivated or redeployed somewhere else in the world. The 3d Tactical Fighter Wing, which had flown out of Bien Hoa since 1965, was gone. The 12th TFW had operated from Cam Ranh Bay also since 1965. It was inactivated in November 1971. The 31st TFW from Tuy Hoa had been sent back to the States. The 35th and 37th TFW were inactivated. The 355th TFW, which had flown so many Thud strikes against the North, was inactivated.

The NVA's Easter offensive began on Good Friday morning, 31 March 1972. Three divisions supported by hundreds of tanks pushed through the DMZ against slight resistance and roared southward. Their objectives: Quang Tri City and then Hue.

Four days later and far to the south, NVA forces rolled across the border from Cambodia into Binh Long Province northwest of Saigon. They quickly

INSIDE VIEW:
The cockpit of an A-37. The pilot sits in the left-hand seat, with the gunsight bolted to the top of the instrument panel, rather as an afterthought, in this modified trainer. Engine instruments are in the center, under the windscreen pillar. The dials in front of each seat are flight instruments: altimeter and artificial horizon and airspeed indicators.

Night gunships

ON THE TRAIL:
The recon photo shows a truck convoy in the Mu Gia pass, one of the key choke points on the Ho Chi Minh Trail out of North Vietnam and into Laos. Around the trail is a wasteland of dead vegetation and fallen trees, caused by defoliants and endless bombing raids.

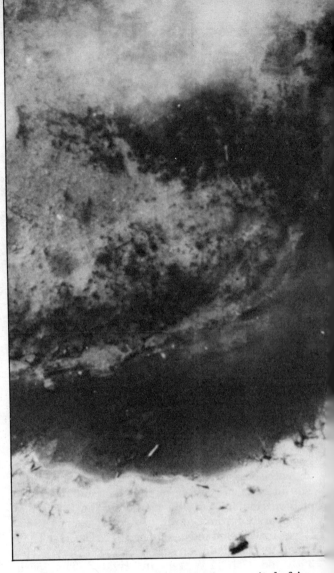

surrounded Loc Ninh and the province capital of An Loc, and took over the airfield at Quan Loi. The remnants of ARVN units and the American advisers at Loc Ninh had to melt away into the jungle and then make their way on foot to An Loc, which was soon under siege.

President Nixon's first response was to resume the bombing of North Vietnam, abandoned by LBJ three and a half years earlier. At first he restricted the strikes to below the 18th Parallel, but soon

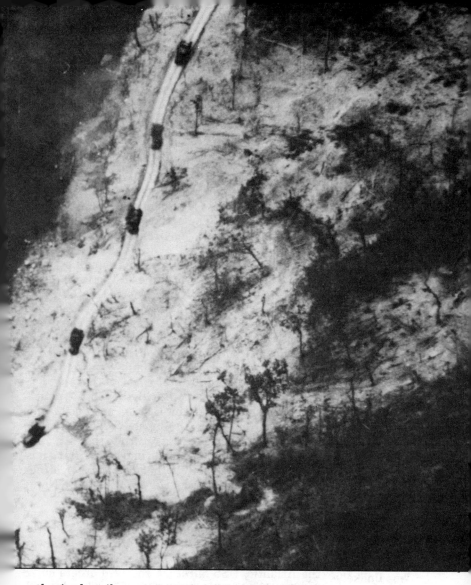

authorized strikes against the rail yard and fuel
storage tanks at Vinh. B-52s struck and cut the rail
lines, but the storage tanks remained intact. Other
B-52 strikes in the next few days moved northward.
They hit Haiphong's fuel storage area and the
Thanh Hoa area.

The bombing did not affect Hanoi's timetable for
invasion. On 23 April, they opened a third front of
the Easter Offensive, striking with two divisions
through the Central Highlands toward Kontum. As

NORTH VIETNAM

Commando hunt area

Mu Gia Pass

Ban Karai Pass

LAOS

SOUTH VIETNAM

Lao Bao Pass

——— Primary road

············· Secondary road

☐ Main gate area

Hard to hit —This map of Commando Hunt target areas demonstrates the reality of the Ho Chi Minh Trail. It was not a single jungle highway, but a complex network of roads and tracks that was hard to cut by aerial bombardment. The so-called "gate" areas were mountain passes where the trails converged, but with four to choose from it was unlikely that the flow of supplies could be stopped completely.

before, air power enabled the South Vietnamese to begin to build an effective defense against the triple onslaught. The American aircraft remaining in the war zone immediately began flying day and night to blunt the advance of the armored columns. The NVA committed several thousand Soviet tanks to the offensive, supported by thousands more armored personnel carriers, mobile AAA guns, and mobile surface-to-air missiles. The air-to-ground situation for the strike aircraft was "target-rich," as the airmen put it. The difference this time was that the multiple NVA targets also had modern air defense weapons. The strike aircraft themselves became a "target-rich" environment for the SAM-2 and AAA gunners.

Units were recalled to Vietnam from all over the world to help stem the tide. The 3d Tactical Fighter Wing was at Kunsan, Korea. Alerted on Saturday, 1 April, the F-4D Phantoms of its 35th Tactical Fighter Squadron were in action only four days later. By 11 April, another 36 F-4D and E Phantoms were flown from Seymour-Johnson AFB to begin operating from bases in Thailand. Twelve F-105G Wild Weasels were also returned to the fray.

On the same day (5 April) the 35th Tactical Fighter Squadron went into action, and two Marine F-4 squadrons back in Japan (VMFA-115 and VMFA-232) were alerted to return to the war. They arrived at Da Nang on 6 April, and began flying missions three days later. Other Marine F-4 attack squadrons launched from Hawaii back to Da Nang, and A-4 squadrons went into Bien Hoa.

The Navy reinforced the carriers *Hancock* and *Coral Sea* promptly, sending *Kitty Hawk* and *Constellation* to the scene by 8 April. USS *Midway* crossed the Pacific to join the fight on 30 April. In the Atlantic, USS *Saratoga* received orders on 28 April to head for the Gulf of Tonkin. Thus by mid-May, six aircraft carriers, each with a wing of 90 aircraft, were on station. During the ensuing campaign, four carriers were active at any one time, with the other two replenishing supplies, undergoing training, or refitting in the Philippines.

The Air Force deployed 108 more F-4D and F-4E Phantoms from US bases to Thailand in mid-May as the NVA offensive continued and the outcome remained in doubt. At the same time, B-52 and

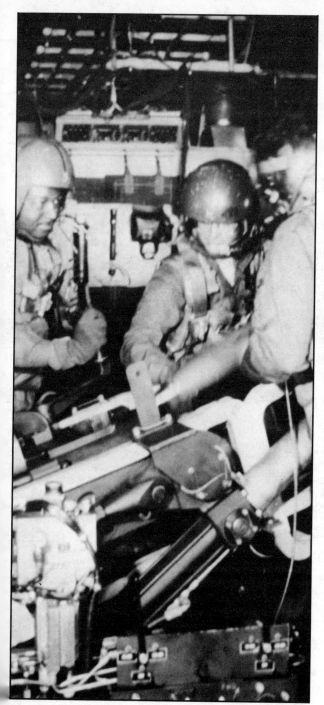

Night gunships

LOAD UP:
A shell slides into the breech of an AC-130H's 105mm gun. At first the gunships would be diverted away from combat areas to make way for "fast-movers" like the F-4, much to the fury of crews; but after a short time, the first question hard-pressed ground troops asked when a gunship arrived overhead was, "Do you have a big gun?"
The guns were synchronized with the sensors: No human aiming skills were needed once the target had been selected on screen.

KC-135 tanker forces were expanded. In April and May, 171 B-52 bombers and 168 KC-135 tankers were added to the strike power.

In the northern I Corps Tactical Zone (ICTZ), the NVA juggernaut rolled toward Quang Tri City. Thousands of air strikes controlled by USAF forward air controllers blasted the NVA armored units. Besides the heavy AAA gun and SA-2 SAM threat, friendly aircraft now had to face the brand-new SA-7 STRELA shoulder-fired air defense missile.

Night gunships

NIGHT BIRD:
An AC-130 in a revetment at Udon, Thailand. Invisible at night, the ultra-black finish is about the most conspicuous possible in daytime, and like Count Dracula, crews hated to find themselves out in the open sky—or anywhere near an NVA antiaircraft gunner—when dawn broke. Only in an environment of total air superiority, and relatively light ground-to-air threat, could such a slow, large weapons platform be used.

Although Western intelligence knew about the new SA-7, this was its first use in combat. A heat-seeker launched from a man's shoulder, the SA-7 was deadly in the Easter Offensive, bringing down several A-1, O-2, and OV-10 aircraft in April (in June, an SA-7 also claimed the first kill of an AC-130 Specter gunship southwest of Hue).

Despite the heavy air support, by 1 May the ARVN commanders in Quang Tri City gave up hope and issued evacuation orders. The disheartened

Freedom fighter —The Northrop F-5 supplied to the VNAF was derived from the USAF's T-38 Talon trainer. A light tactical fighter, it was capable of supersonic flight, powered by two non-afterburning General Electric J85 turbojets. The F-5A was a single-seat aircraft; the F-5B in this shelter at Bien Hoa had two seats in tandem for training. Its maximum military load was 6,200 pounds. It could mount two AIM-9 Sidewinder air-to-air missiles, bombs, rockets, and napalm.

troops panicked and fled southward toward Hue. A senior FAC, Lieutenant Colonel Ray E. Stratton, described the scene: "It was an appalling sight. There was just a complete litter of US built armored personnel carriers, tanks, and trucks. In the rice fields off to the east of the highway (Highway 1) you could see where the tanks and APCs had run out of gas. They were abandoned in twos and threes."

Near Hue, the ARVN leadership finally regained control of its troops. Galvanized by new leadership and American fire support, they held firm. Good flying weather returned in the first week of May. Hundreds of NVA tanks and armored vehicles were destroyed, both by South Vietnamese armored units and thousands of USAF, Navy, and Marine air strikes. The enemy's advance was halted by early May.

Of the hundreds of battles fought during the Easter Offensive, the siege of An Loc stands out. An Loc, the capital of Binh Long Province, was one of the jump-off points for the invasion of Cambodia two years earlier. Control of it and Highway 13 would give the NVA forces a straight shot down the highway into Saigon, just 100 kilometers south. More than three NVA divisions besieged the town from April 7 to June 9.

Round-the-clock air cover was flown by VNAF F-5s and A-1s, plus A-6 Intruders and A-7 Corsair IIs from USS *Constellation*, and US Air Force A-37 Dragonflies, F-4 Phantoms, and AC-130 Spectre gunships.

The NVA and regular Viet Cong formations were supported by Soviet-built T-54 tanks, heavy 155mm howitzers, and 122mm rockets for the ground attack. For air defense, they had guns ranging from 12.7mm up to 57mm, plus the deadly new SA-7s. As they pushed closer into the town, the Communist troops built reinforced bunkers and firing positions. From them they pounded the town with up to 2,000 shells per day. For the 20,000 persons inside An Loc, conditions quickly became horrific.

Resupply was totally by air. But the Communist missiles and AAA were so intense that daylight drops had to be curtailed. Nighttime parachute drops of supplies and ammunition landed on a soccer field about 200 meters square. Even so, C-130 airlifters, trying for accuracy by dropping from low

level, were hit. High-level drops with new equipment and techniques were developed and succeeded in keeping supplies up to a minimum sustenance level.

On one occasion all the B-52 strikes planned for South Vietnam were diverted to break up an NVA attack, streaming tons of bombs in succession on the waves of enemy troops, who were seen running in panic.

The AC-119K Stinger and AC-130 Spectre gunships were critical to the successful defense of An Loc. Both types carried the multiple sensors such as infrared and low-light collectors for night operations. They both mounted ranks of fast-firing (6,000 rounds per minute) 7.62mm and 20mm Gatling guns. And now the AC-130s had an additional punch. An Army 105mm howitzer was part of the AC-130's armament, rigged to fire its heavy ammunition directly into hardened targets.

The AC-130's precision capabilities soon became

LIVE SHOW:
A Spectre crewman monitors his infrared display. The infrared sensors scanning the ground below were accurate enough to detect even the heat from a cup of coffee.

Night gunships

FATAL FIRE:
An AC-130 blazes on the runway at Udon. Two men died when the Spectre was hit over Laos. Pilot Colonel William Schwehm nursed the bird home despite having neither rudder nor elevator controls. Nearing the base, he ordered non-essential crew members to bail out. On landing, the plane made it some 2,000 feet down the runway before it veered to the right and lost a wing. The gunship burst into flames as the pilot, copilot, and navigator/sensor operator safely evacuated. Those who bailed out were rescued.

familiar to the US Army advisers inside An Loc, especially when the Communist forces got into the town and began firing from buildings.

So precise were the AC-130's armaments that one US adviser recalls asking an AC-130 for fire on a fountain that was easily identifiable. The AC-130 hit the fountain. The adviser next asked for a burst of fire at a street intersection two blocks east. The AC-130 hit it. Then he identified a particular house nearby. Heavy firing was coming from it and hitting friendly forces across the street. The adviser asked the AC-130 to destroy the house. It did so

immediately and precisely, with 20mm, 40mm, and 105mm fire.

The gunships, B-52s, and other strike aircraft saved An Loc. On 9 June, the attackers started to withdraw. The Easter Offensive was over, although diminished fighting continued through the summer. NVA losses were extraordinary, estimated at more than 100,000 killed. But the enemy held part of South Vietnam to 10 kilometers below the DMZ. More important, the NVA controlled a chunk of the country astride Highway 13, a permanent menace to Saigon.

Back to Hanoi

Bombing the sanctuaries

IN THE bomb-free period of three and a half years from 1 November 1968 to 30 March 1972, Hanoi and its suppliers rebuilt the internal lines of communication of North Vietnam, and modernized its forces. Bridges and rail lines were rebuilt, and the port capacity of Haiphong increased. MiG-17 interceptors were reinforced by 33 MiG-19 and 93 top-line MiG-21s. Pilots of the interceptor fleet were intensively trained. Jet-serviceable airfields numbered 16, up from 5 in 1967. Coverage of ground control intercept radars was expanded, as was the area covered by surface-to-air missiles.

In response to the massive North Vietnamese Easter Offensive, President Nixon dispatched Navy, Air Force, and Marine aircraft back to Southeast Asia. Beginning on 6 April 1972 he first authorized limited strikes south of the 18th Parallel. When the NVA offensive rolled on, he moved the strikes northward. B-52s struck targets at Vinh and then in the Than Hoa and Haiphong areas. Twelve F-4s of the 8th Tactical Fighter Wing struck the Thanh Hoa bridge on 27 April. Five electro-optical guided bombs damaged the bridge, but could not drop it.

When the NVA offensive continued for more than a month and Hanoi showed no indications of seeking a cease-fire, President Nixon took additional steps. On 8 May, he suspended the peace talks in Paris and authorized mining of harbors, including Haiphong. North Vietnam's formidable air defense system was about to get a workout against swarms of real targets: the bombers of the Linebacker I campaign.

Linebacker I was intended to interdict and destroy North Vietnam's transportation system, and curtail the flow of supplies into the country and to its forces

Back to Hanoi

CRASH LANDING: Smoke pours from a Marine F-4 after a belly landing at Da Nang due to combat damage to the main undercarriage. Fire tenders are spraying the underside to stop the fire from spreading, but are trying not to wreck the rest of the aircraft by avoiding flooding the cockpit and nose electronics.

fighting in South Vietnam. Rolling Thunder, with similar objectives, had not achieved its goals. The strikes were too limited in nature and too tightly controlled from Washington. In Linebacker I, the situation was different, and the bombing campaign more intensive. Attack sorties during Linebacker I reached 15,000 per month.

First, the ports were closed by sowing mines. Naval aviation took care of that task in just over an hour on the morning of 8 May in a tightly

coordinated operation. Grumman A-6 Intruders from three aircraft carriers sowed the mines, and closed six ports, including Haiphong, the biggest.

The mining of North Vietnam's harbors was years late. Once the ports had been the main source of supplies. Now an extensive road and rail net existed from South China into North Vietnam. The Soviet Union and China would be forced to divert supplies that way, rather than continue shipping through Haiphong. Late or not, the mining had its effects.

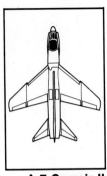

**A-7 Corsair II
(Vought) (LTV)
USN, USAF
—One of several
aircraft
developed by
the Navy, then
adopted by the
Air Force. A
single-jet,
subsonic attack
aircraft with
very advanced
navigation and
strike avionics,
the A-7A was
first used in
Southeast Asia
in December
1967, flying
from USS
Ranger. An Air
Force A-7D of
354th Tactical
Fighter Wing
flew the last
strike mission in
Southeast Asia,
on 15 August
1973.**

Enough mines of various types were laid to ensure that Haiphong and the other ports were unapproachable. North Vietnam did not attempt to disarm or sweep the mines. Twenty-seven cargo ships were trapped inside Haiphong harbor, stuck there until the cease-fire nearly a year later. Within ten days the North Vietnamese were running short of ammunition, the US Seventh Fleet commander reported.

To choke off movement of supplies within North Vietnam and cut its shipments to its invading forces in the South, hundreds of bridges, rebuilt since Rolling Thunder, had to be dropped again. Among them were, of course, the Paul Doumer bridge in downtown Hanoi, and the massive Thanh Hoa bridge that had withstood so many previous strikes.

US aircraft and weapons technology had advanced considerably since these targets were last attacked. New aircraft included the latest Phantom, the F-4E, and the Navy's A-6 Intruder and A-7 Corsair II. There was also the experience factor; the results of earlier operations had been thoroughly evaluated and better tactics and techniques had been devised.

Among the new weapons were electro-optical guided bombs (EOGB) and laser guided bombs (LGB). Both types were heavy bombs, in the 2,000- to 3,000-pound range (the Thanh Hoa bridge showed that ultraheavy bombs were needed), and both were precision-guided.

At the start of Linebacker I, the strike forces had smarter pilots, smarter aircraft, and smarter bombs to send against the formidable air defenses of North Vietnam. In addition, many strike aircraft were now equipped with electronic countermeasures equipment and dispensers for chaff to confuse air defense radars.

At the peak rate of 15,000 per month, nearly 100,000 sorties were flown by Air Force, Navy, and Marine aircraft during Linebacker I. No targets were easy. Given the improved state of air defense, both in the North and with the invasion units in the South, the flying was more hazardous than before. But the strike forces achieved results. The Linebacker strikes slowed the flow of supplies into South Vietnam, blunted the invasion, and by the end of the campaign in October 1972, were credited with convincing Hanoi to resume peace talks. The 8th

Tactical Fighter Wing would make many of the key strikes in the renewed campaign. Based at Ubon, Thailand, since December 1965, the 8th TFW was nicknamed "MiG-Killers," for the high number of kills made by its aircrews during Rolling Thunder. Now the 8th was equipped with newer F-4Ds and F-4Es, along with the smart bombs. By the end of June 1972, the wing had a new nickname, "Bridge Busters." Its crews had destroyed 106 bridges, including both the Paul Doumer and the Thanh Hoa.

Colonel Carl S. Miller led the 8th TFW against the Paul Doumer bridge in Hanoi on 10 May 1972.

Targets for the day also included the Yen Bien rail yards. Colonel Miller led the part of his wing committed against the bridge. Sixteen of the wing's F-4Es were loaded with 2,000-pound guided bombs. Eight other F-4s were committed to provide chaff support. Flak suppression would be flown by 15 F-105G Wild Weasels from the 388th TFW at Korat, which would also provide four EB-66 electronic

HARBOR BAR: The main channel into Haiphong Harbor was closed in a single day with mines dropped by six A-7 Corsair IIs and three A-6 Intruders from the carrier *Coral Sea* without the loss of any planes, despite Haiphong's well-organized air defenses.

Back to Hanoi

ELECTRIC WARRIOR: A Marine EA-6A electronic warfare aircraft refuelling on the ground. The EA-6 carried a crew of four, two more than the standard A-6, including two electronic warfare specialists to run the fat packages of detection and jamming gear, two of which are visible on top of the tail fin and on the wing behind the ground crewman in this picture. Note the windmill electricity generator on the front of the wing pod. The EA-6A carried more than 30 ECM antennas to confuse enemy radio and radar transmissions.

countermeasures aircraft. Takeoff time for the chaff aircraft was 0800 hours. The 8th TFW strike aircraft would launch 20 minutes later.

Colonel Charles A. Gabriel's 432d Tactical Reconnaissance Wing from Udorn was committed to high cover against MiGs and post-strike reconnaissance. Navy aviation was committed also. The air wings from *Constellation*, *Coral Sea*, and *Kitty Hawk* were assigned to targets in the Hanoi and Haiphong areas. From *Kitty Hawk*, 37 A-6 Intruders and A-7E Corsair IIs struck the Hai Duong bridge, a key link

between Hanoi and Haiphong. This was an all-out effort, designed to overload and overwhelm the air defenses.

On time at 0800 hours, the chaff aircraft lifted off the runway at Ubon and headed north, first for refueling and then to lay down the corridors of chaff that would confound the enemy radars. Twenty minutes later, Colonel Miller led the 16 F-4Es of the strike force off the runway at Ubon. They flew in flights of four, each composed of two elements of two aircraft. Three flights carried laser guided bombs;

Phantom base —Maintenance crews make the final instrument checks on a flight of F-4 Phantoms in the revetments at Ubon air base in Thailand, where 76 USAF Phantoms were stationed. During the Linebacker campaigns of 1972 these Phantoms flew night and day missions against North Vietnam.

one flight was loaded with electro-optical guided bombs.

Captain Mike Messett led one of the two-ship LGB-armed elements. This mission was his second time at the Paul Doumer bridge. He was in the strike force the first time the bridge was hit, back in August 1967. That time, he was a backseater. AAA hit his aircraft, exploding up front and wounding the aircraft commander. Mike Messett recovered the aircraft, and flew it from the backseat. He made an emergency in-flight refueling, nursed the plane back to Ubon, and made a successful rear-seat landing. Now he was flying from the front seat, leading a flight of four Phantoms.

The southwest monsoon had clouded over the bases in Thailand. But as the swarms of strike and support aircraft refueled and crossed the mountains into the far north, the weather cleared.

The chaff aircraft flew in first, creating a protective corridor for the final run by the strike aircraft. But the defenses were still vigorous. Colonel Miller remembers how at 40 miles out they ran into SAMs: "They stayed with us all the way in. Over Hanoi (we) encountered extremely heavy AAA. The sky was black with 100, 85, and 37mm antiaircraft fire, in addition to the SAMs coming up to meet us. Perhaps 130 SAMs were launched at us in those brief minutes. Five of them came right up through the middle of my flight. On the road back out, however, it was largely AAA and MiGs. Two MiGs showed up and fired a few missiles before pulling out."

A total of 160 SAMs were launched at the strike force, and 41 MiG interceptors tried to stop the strikes. The high cover force of USAF and Navy F-4s killed eleven MiGs (seven MiG-21s and four MiG-17s) at a cost of four Phantoms.

Captain Messett and his wingman joined up with the lead element of their flight. They closed up to within four ship widths of each other. The flight leader rolled the four Phantoms toward the bridge and illuminated the target with laser energy. At 14,000 feet he released his LGBs. That was the cue for Messett's element to drop theirs into the "basket" created by the leader's laser.

The multiple blasts of the 2,000-pound EOGBs and LGBs created a pall of smoke that obscured the target. Seven EOGBs and 22 LGBs were dropped on

BRIDGE OFF ABUTMENT

BREAKS IN SPAN

the bridge. The crews reported 12 direct hits, and 4 probables. Colonel Miller recalled, "When we decided to come home, we left the tracks cut, about 1,000 feet of roadway on one side and 300 feet on the other side sitting in the water." Reconnaissance photos proved the success of the mission. One span was completely destroyed and several others damaged. Once again, rail traffic from Hanoi to the southern cities was cut.

The rail line between Hanoi and Haiphong was also cut. The Navy strike on the Hai Duong bridge was flown by A-6 Intruders of VA-52, plus two squadrons of A-7Es (VA-192 and VA-195). Despite walls of flak and SAMs flying everwhere, the attackers pressed through.

For the American prisoners of war suffering under Hanoi's brutal treatment, the strikes on May 10 were a tonic. For three and a half years, they had not heard the roar of jet engines or the *crump* of bombs. They had no news of activities outside their senses. It appeared that they had been abandoned. Now, however, US airpower was back with a vengeance, and their morale shot up.

To make sure the Paul Doumer bridge stayed

BROKEN JAW:

The infamous Dragon's Jaw bridge was left a shattered wreck after the raid of 13 May 1972. The single successful attack on one of North Vietnam's key strategic communications assets by F-4Es of 334th Squadron, after some 700 previous unsuccessful sorties, was the first mission to demonstrate the value of guided weapons.

Back to Hanoi

down, another attack was ordered for the next day, 11 May. Only four aircraft flew the strike, led by Captain Messett. One aircraft carried two 3,000-pound LGBs; each of the other three dropped two 2,000-pound LGBs. Through some mixup, the chaff and MiG cover aircraft flew in early and left before Messett and his flight arrived. No other strikes were in the area.

It was an eerie feeling, to be so alone. Captain Messett thought the SAMs would have an easy time, but although a few were launched, none hit the four Phantoms. No MiGs came up either. Apparently the small force and chaff mixup confused the North Vietnamese as much as it concerned the attackers. Captain Messett said, "I think the North Vietnamese couldn't believe what was going on."

Messett selected a span on the Hanoi side, rolled in, and released his bombs. On his signal his flight members dropped all their bombs tracking toward

the target Messett was illuminating. They flew out
of the area unscathed. The small force achieved
phenomenal results: Their eight LGBs dropped three
more spans into the water and damaged three
others. The bridge was out of commission for
months. On 10 September, a day of rare clear
weather, four F-4s of the 8th TFW hit it one last
time, dropping two more spans.

On 13 May, it was the turn of the Thanh Hoa
bridge. By the time of this mission the 8th Tactical
Fighter Wing had been reinforced by a squadron of
F-4Es, the 334th, from Seymour-Johnson AFB,
North Carolina.

They were tagged to bring down the Thanh Hoa
bridge on 13 May. Colonel Richard G. Horne, the 8th
TFW's deputy commander for operations, would lead
the strike. The strike force was sixteen F-4E aircraft.
The first twelve to hit the bridge would drop eight
3,000-pound and sixteen 2,000-pound LGBs. Right

EB-66 (Douglas) USAF —Air Force version of the A-3 Douglas Skywarrior. Bristling with electronic counter-measures equipment, it proved a formidable weapon. The twin-jet attack aircraft carried a three-man crew, had a maximum bomb capacity of 12,800 pounds, and carried two 20mm cannon.

behind them, a flight of four F-4Es led by Major Thomas E. McNiff would strike with 48 Mk-82 gravity bombs. (McNiff's Blue Flight of four Phantoms was a prudent all-purpose force. If the first 12 aircraft were molested by MiGs, his flight would drop their bombs and fight off the interceptors with AIM-7 Sparrow and AIM-9 Sidewinder missiles, and their internal 20-mm cannon. If the weather over the bridge closed down, preventing use of the LGBs, the 48 MK-82s from Blue Flight would inflict some damage and make the flight worthwhile.)

The sixteen Phantoms roared off the Ubon runway on schedule for their rendezvous with the Dragon's Jaw at 1400 hours Hanoi time. They joined up with KC-135 tankers over Laos to top off with JP-4 fuel, then streaked straight east across the narrow neck of southern North Vietnam, turned left, and headed north toward the bridge.

Up ahead, the men in the EB-66 electronic countermeasures aircraft watched display scopes and listened through headphones for the telltale indications that SAM and AAA radars were being turned on. Inside the F-4Es, the main background noises in the aircrews' headphones were the sounds of their breathing through the oxygen masks. Those regular tones were interrupted from time to time by the crackle of brief comments on the intercom. The sun shone high behind the strike aircraft. The coastline looked placid and benign, the tranquil view belying the dangers that lay in concealed sites in the green landscape. But also far below clouds began to appear. As the attackers turned in toward the bridge flak bursts rose to meet them. All calibers were firing; from 37mm to 85 and 100mm, the guns roared and SAMs began to fly.

As he led the first flight in, Colonel Horne just got one glimpse of the bridge before the clouds obscured his view. "I pulled up and cleared Three and Four to roll in if they could see the target." They could, and released their bombs. Colonel Horne and his weapons systems officer (WSO) saw six red flashes, which meant the bombs hit something solid. He said, "Then I went back up to make damn sure the rest of the aircraft got in." He cleared the rest of the flights to attack.

By now, all of the defenses were blazing away at the attacking Phantoms, with the intensity increasing as each flight of four attacked the bridge. Major Tom McNiff led the last four Phantoms through the flak, smoke, and clouds to drop their 500-pounders. In the face of massive fires, he pressed his attack to drop his flight's bombs. Large clouds of dust were rising and flashes of fire from exploding bombs hampered their vision, but they bored right in, blasting the span.

A gap appeared in the clouds and a breeze moved the smoke aside. Colonel Horne said, "Suddenly, for one brief second, I caught sight of the bridge again. I couldn't believe my eyes—it appeared to be in the water!" It was indeed. Reconnaissance photos taken by an RF-4C a few minutes after the strike confirmed the strike pilots' impressions: The bridge's superstructure was twisted and cut, and the western span had been knocked clear off its 40-foot-thick concrete abutment.

Last man in —Tom McNiff's Blue Flight of F-4Es, dropping conventional Mark-82 "iron bombs" were the last aircraft over Thanh Hoa bridge before it finally fell.

General John W. Vogt, commander of Seventh Air Force, congratulated the aircrews of the 8th TFW who made the attack. "The Thanh Hoa bridge, which has been a fighter pilot's nemesis for seven years, is down in the water. Many hundreds of sorties have been expended and more than 30 aircraft have been lost over the past six years in attempts to accomplish this feat. You have done what no one else has been able to do."

As always, the North Vietnamese immediately pressed repair efforts on the bridge. Periodic strikes were laid on throughout the summer to hamper the work and keep the bridge unusable. Naval aviators struck it eleven more times and Air Force crews struck twice more before October 23, when President Nixon halted bombing of North Vietnam.

The thousands of air strikes flown during Linebacker I accomplished the objectives President Nixon wanted. On 29 June, he said, "The situation has been completely turned around." Once again, he called for an international cease-fire and the return of US POWs.

Peace talks resumed in Paris on 13 July. Linebacker strikes continued through the summer, keeping pressure on the leadership in Hanoi.

The Paris talks seemed to produce movement toward a cease-fire. On October 23, President Nixon halted all bombing north of the 20th Parallel. Was peace at hand, as Henry Kissinger proclaimed?

Uncle Sam goes to war

9.

B-52s over Hanoi

THE SELF-IMPOSED cease-fire of Linebacker I had lasted barely two months before the heaviest bombing campaign in history, Linebacker II, began. Captain Jon A. Reynolds had been a POW held in Hanoi for more than seven years when the Linebacker II raids began.

He said: "For the first time, the United States was really going to war . . . the guards, some openly weeping, simply headed for their shelters—individual manholes—and pulled concrete lids over their heads. This was our proudest moment."

Another prisoner, Major Leo Thorsness, remembers the night of 18 December 1972 as the happiest night of his life: "I jumped out from under my mosquito net to watch and hear perhaps the most spectacular bombardment in history." At that time he did not know that he had been awarded the Medal of Honor for his courage in a Wild Weasel F-105 back in 1967.

During the "Eleven-Day War" of December 18 through 29, B-52s in concert with hundreds of other aircraft blasted Hanoi with an intensity unmatched in earlier raids such as Rolling Thunder. The campaign of days and nights of relentless raids was christened Linebacker II. Linebacker I began in May 1972, and ended on 23 October when President Nixon suspended bombing north of the 20th Parallel. But the POWs did not know of events in Washington or at the Paris peace talks. They were cut off from information.

The genesis of Linebacker II came on December 13, when the North Vietnamese delegation walked out of the Paris peace talks. President Nixon and Dr. Kissinger wanted to regain Hanoi's attention.

President Nixon ordered the bombing of military

Uncle Sam goes to war

TABS ON CHARLIE: A USAF EB-66 electronic warfare plane, bristling with tiny antennas. Navy and Air Force ECM ships took up position before the Linebacker II missions for an unprecedented electronic onslaught on the North Vietnamese radar and communications networks. Air Force F-4s dropped corridors of chaff, thin strips of tin foil that floated slowly to the ground, to confuse enemy radar. Other F-4s flew high cover in case MiGs got aloft. Air Force F-105Gs and Navy A-7Es were to launch their antiradar homing missiles against the SAMs' radar.

targets in Hanoi, Haiphong, and nearby areas. The Joint Chiefs of Staff directed the Strategic Air Command (SAC) to mount a maximum effort. Using B-52 bombers, SAC was to strike war-supporting complexes in the Hanoi and Haiphong areas, and along important lines of logistics. SAC was also instructed to take every precaution to minimize civilian casualties and avoid damage to third-country shipping in the Haiphong port.

The warning order reached Andersen Air Force Base on Guam and U-Tapao Air Base in Thailand late on December 15.

Targets for the B-52 bombers were 34 complexes in Hanoi, Haiphong, Thai Nguyen, Kep, Bac Giang, and Lang Dang areas, with the majority in the vicinity of Hanoi. For the first time, air bases would be struck ahead of the raid time to suppress the MiG-21 interceptors. SAM sites and support complexes would also be hit. To the pilots it was about time; until now those air bases and SAM sites had been restricted from strikes by Washington.

Preceding and accompanying the B-52s would be the Air Force's new F-111 Aardvark fighter-bomber and the Navy's A-6 Intruder. Those two aircraft

Ground target —A USAF reconnaissance photo of two Soviet-built MiG-17 jet fighters in their protective shelter at Phuc Yen airfield. A critical element in North Vietnam's air defenses, the MiGs were prime targets for the strike aircraft sent in advance of the B-52 bombers.

possessed true night attack equipment, and carried heavy bomb loads. In daytime, targets requiring precision would be hit by attack aircraft from the Navy carriers in Task Force 77 off the coast and by Air Force strike aircraft from Thailand. The idea was to use "smart bombs" in day strikes on point targets, and regular iron bombs from B-52s on area targets at night. (As it happened, the weather over North Vietnam was poor during the entire period of Linebacker II. Only twelve hours of suitable clear daylight occurred during the eleven-day campaign. The day strike aircraft used the short period to advantage, blasting targets such as Radio Hanoi with precision.)

The plan for Linebacker II called for three nights of bombing, then a pause to gauge results. B-52s committed the first night were 42 D models from U-Tapao, plus 54 B-52G and 33 D models from Andersen; a total of 129. They would attack in three waves, with four to five hours between waves. The first wave was to hit at 1945 hours, the second near midnight, and the third just before dawn.

For all strikes, it was imperative to interfere with the enemy's electronics capabilities. The North Vietnamese used radio and radar to detect and control their forces of MiGs, SAMs, and AAA guns. Electronic warfare aircraft from the Navy, Marine Corps, and Air Force remained on station for all strikes to carry out the electronic countermeasures (ECM) missions.

Round-trip flying time for the B-52s from Andersen AFB was up to 16 hours; for those from U-Tapao, the trip could be flown in four. By the time the last crews from Guam struck the targets and landed back at Andersen, the first wave of the second day's strikes would be taking off. This meant that the second day's crews would not have the benefit of debriefings of the first crews.

The Guam-based aircraft flew westward, refueled from tankers based on Okinawa, then continued westward to landfall on the coast of South Vietnam. They turned northward over Cambodia and Laos, joining up with the force from U-Tapao.

As night fell over North Vietnam, the long stream of B-52s in the first wave was inbound to its targets. Captain Robert E. Wolff, flying one of the first B-52s from Guam, recalled the flight: "We flew on north

Uncle Sam goes to war

AARDVARK:
An F-111 on the way to strike Hanoi's air defenses, swing wings set half forward for a medium-hard ride from the terrain-following radar. Missions were flown alone, blind, simply relying on electronics to navigate and fly the ship through the mountains. One surprised aviator described arriving over Hanoi one evening to find the city lit up "like Las Vegas." Suddenly block after block was plunged into darkness as sirens howled and power station switches were thrown.

135

almost to the border of China before turning back south down the Red River Valley . . . This route into Hanoi was terribly familiar to American fighter-bomber pilots. It was the same one used during the raids of 1965-68. It was also familiar to the North Vietnamese. Sixty-seven B-52s flying down the Red River one behind the other was not exactly our idea of the best way into the target area. SAMs were fired at the bomber stream in a shotgun pattern. The Vietnamese simply tripped off salvos of six missiles from each site. From the beginning of the bomb run

Uncle Sam goes to war

TARGET CITY: This aerial photo of Hanoi shows military targets selected for Linebacker, including Gia Lam airfield (No. 1), the thermal power plant (2), and railroad yards (3 and 4). Number 5, outlined in white, is the "Hanoi Hilton," where American POWs, many of them airmen, were held. Number 6, in the next block, is the Cuban chancellery, which was accidently hit by bombs. At every stage of the campaign, military commanders and political leaders had to answer accusations that they were hitting civilian targets.

to the target, my gunner counted 32 SAMs fired at or at least passing near our aircraft."

By changing tactics, the North Vietnamese SAM controllers were frustrating the ECM aircraft. The EB-66 and F-105s jammed the SAM guidance radars. In reaction, the Vietnamese salvoed six SAMs at a time from each active site, detonating them at the calculated altitude of the B-52 stream. The B-52s' known routes and formation in a 70-mile column made the task easy for the defenders.

The U-Tapao wave struck first, with 108 bombs

Antimissile —The Standard ARM (antiradar missile) was carried by the Wild Weasels during Linebacker II. Designed as a successor to the Shrike as the basic anti-radiation missile, the Standard had a range of 35 miles, 25 miles longer than the Shrike, and a bigger warhead.

dropping from each of its B-52Ds. Its bombs blasted MiG bases at Hoa Lac, Kep, and Phuc Yen from high altitude using radar. F-111s from Takhli hit the MiG bases with precision radar bombing at ultralow level. One of the few MIG-21s that took to the air was shot down by Staff Sergeant Samuel O. Turner, tail gunner in Brown 3, a B-52D.

The waves of B-52s from Guam followed, hitting rail yards and storage areas.

Three B-52s were lost on the first night, two Gs from Andersen and one D from U-Tapao. Both G models were hit by SAMs a few seconds before bomb release. The crew of one G, led by Lieutenant Colonel Hendsley R. Conner, was able to nurse the flaming bird 250 miles across the Thai border. They bailed out successfully, and were rescued. The crew of the other G was less fortunate. The commander and a gunner were killed by the SAM, and three other crew members ejected over Hanoi and were captured. The sixth man was missing in action.

Similar routes and tactics were flown on the second and third nights. The crews did not like flying routes very much like those flown the nights before; they were too easy for the defenders. Besides disliking the routes, many of the crew members criticized the "post-target turn." They believed that making the prescribed turn immediately after bomb release made a better target for the SAM radars. They advocated continued level flight with maximum use of electronic countermeasures until the aircraft were out of the heavy threat area.

Although SAMs, MiGs, and AAA fire were heavy on the second night, there were no B-52 losses. The SAC top command decided to use the same routes and attack plan on the third night, 20 December. The B-52s flew in three waves again, using the same narrow approach route out of the northwest down to Hanoi. Nine cells (27 B-52s) were to hit the Yen Vien rail yard again. SAM fires from there were light on the preceding night. Not so this time. The SAMs were ready, helped by the MiGs. The MiG fighters flew alongside the B-52 stream, reporting altitude, airspeed, and heading to the SAM controllers. They launched salvos of SAMs into the bomber stream without using the normal guidance signals. Immune to electronic countermeasures and set to detonate at precisely the right altitude, the

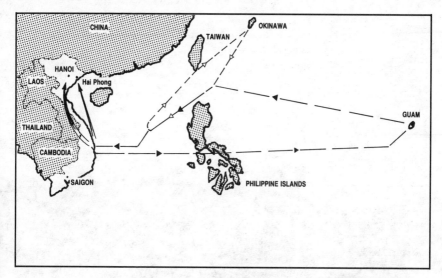

SAMs were effective. The third aircraft in the leading cell of three bombers was called Quilt 3. It was blasted in the post-target turn.

A pilot in the following cell, Captain Rolland Scott, saw what happened:

"(The SAMs) arrived in pairs, just a few seconds apart. Some, as they passed, would explode—a few close enough to shake my aircraft. I could see SAM activity ahead in the vicinity of the target. In fact, while on the run we saw a large ball of fire erupt some few miles ahead of us, and slowly turn to the right and descend. I thought it was a BUFF (Big Ugly Fat Fella—Guam Pidgin for a B-52), and was sure no one would survive what was apparently a direct hit. I later learned what I saw was Quilt 3 going down in flames. Amazingly, four crew members successfully ejected."

Quilt 3 was a G model. Aircraft of the fourth cell, designated Brass, were also Gs. Brass 2 was hit while making the same post-target turn. The damage was bad, but the crew was able to nurse the crippled aircraft across the Thai border before bailing out. Two more cells got through without hits. But Orange 3, a D model, was hit seconds before bomb release and exploded over the target.

Word of these losses flashed like a shock wave back to Andersen, U-Tapao, and SAC headquarters. Should the succeeding waves, already launched, continue to the targets, or should they be recalled?

BOEINGS REUNION:
The awesome scale of Linebacker II meant that the refuelling effort by KC-135 tankers had to be run from a base separate from the big bombers. It took a B-52 between 15 and 20 minutes to take on 100,000 pounds of fuel, a stressful time for pilots, who were aware that one slip could mean a disastrous collision. They aimed to fly precisely enough to fill up without a single disconnection.

General John C. Meyer, SAC commander, made the decision: Press on.

The second wave, coming in four hours behind the first, had no losses or damage.

The third wave, aimed against high-priority military targets, headed down the same well-traveled route in the airway northwest of Hanoi. Its attack was a nightmare. A D model was hit first, while making its post-target turn. Its crew managed to get as far as northern Laos before abandoning the aircraft.

Eight minutes later, a G model was hit on the turn. The pilot, Lieutenant Colonel Jim Nagahiro, and the navigator, Captain Lynn Beens, were captured. Lieutenant Colonel Keith Heggen was riding in the aircraft as deputy commander of the raid. He was wounded and died in prison. The other crew

members were lost. The nightmare was not yet over. Six planes back was another G model with malfunctioning radar equipment, called Tan 3. Tan 3 became separated from its cellmates, and was easy meat for the SAMs. One exploded underneath the aircraft, crippling it. While the crew struggled to get the B-52G back under control, another SAM hit it. Only one crew member, Staff Sergeant Jim Lollar, lived. He became a POW.

Night Three was over, at an intolerable cost: four G models and two D models were down, and a third D was damaged. Obviously the battle plan was defective. Although the MiGs were not causing much damage, the North Vietnamese seemed to have plenty of SAMs left. More than 220 were shot on Night Three, hitting seven aircraft, of which six were lost. In addition to defective tactics, some of

Control center —A backward-writing plotter jots down new data on a transparent status board at Seventh Air Force's tactical air control center, Tan Son Nhut. The airspace of Vietnam was usually busier than that of the continental US.

the equipment fell short of need. About half of the Gs had modified electronic countermeasures packages. Most of the Gs shot down were from the unmodified half. It was past time to appraise the situation and develop solutions. Furthermore, the word came from Washington that the campaign would be carried on indefinitely.

SAC could not do that for long by losing six aircraft nightly, or even three. The force on Guam got a respite while the reevaluation was under way. It was not used against North Vietnam on Night Four. Instead, it sent 30 aircraft over South Vietnam to train new crews. The night's bombing effort against Hanoi was handled by 30 D-model aircraft from U-Tapao.

The bombing radar in one of the lead aircraft failed just before the release point, and it became separated from its mates. MiGs swooped down on it, but their fires missed. A SAM blasted the aircraft and it was lost.

Five minutes behind, Lieutenant Colonel Bill Conlee was leading Blue Cell. Bomb release time was 0347 hours. As the aircraft reached the initial point for the last few minutes' run in, the copilot, Captain Dave Drummond, said, "It looks like we'll walk on SAMs tonight." He was too right. Ten SAMs exploded near Blue Cell as it approached the release point. When the bombs were released over the target, two SAMs bracketed the aircraft. Four crew members were wounded and the aircraft was mortally damaged. The crew ejected from the doomed aircraft.

Colonel Conlee saw more SAMs passing as he fell through the night, badly wounded. His parachute opened, and he descended into a field. He thought he was alone, but a mob soon set upon him. He was stripped and forced to hobble through a mile-long gauntlet of clubs, farm tools, and bamboo poles. He was dumped into a truck like a sack of potatoes, and held face down on the truckbed.

During the hour's ride, Conlee was able to stem the flow of blood from his wounded face and left arm. The truck stopped in downtown Hanoi as night was fading. He said, "I was then unceremoniously pushed off the truck flatbed, falling about six feet to the pavement, where I suffered a shoulder separation. I was unable to move from where I had landed,

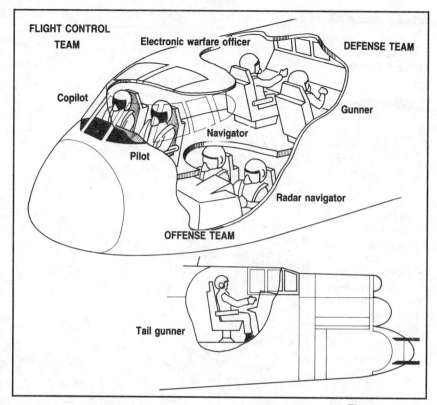

FLIGHT CONTROL TEAM
Electronic warfare officer
DEFENSE TEAM
Copilot
Gunner
Pilot
Navigator
Radar navigator
OFFENSE TEAM
Tail gunner

and was then dragged by two soldiers into the prison yard of what I was to discover was the Hanoi Hilton." He was beaten and kicked for three days before his captors gave up questioning him.

SAC headquarters and the staffs at Guam and U-Tapao threw themselves into a comprehensive review of what was being done wrong. Clearly the tactics were defective. SAC was notorious for centralized control of operations, as in prescribing the single route into Hanoi. Now, however, raid commanders would have authority to vary tactics in light of the situation. The post-target turn was thrown out. Instead, the aircraft would fly out to sea, then turn to head back to base. (Jim McInerney's Wild Weasels had learned five years earlier about the vulnerability of the post-target turn. Now SAC relearned the same lesson, at high cost.)

Routes into the targets were to be varied, a measure applauded by the crews. Also, altitudes would vary, making the SAMs' job harder. Another

TIGHT FIT:
Seating positions for the crew of a B-52G, (above), and the rear gunner's position on the older D model (below). Crews liked to have a man in the back because he could warn of SAM launches on the intercom, avoiding the confusion of warnings over the radio.

Uncle Sam goes to war

OVER THE TARGET:
A cell of three B-52s, in formation for maximum effectiveness of their ECM jammers, at the moment of bomb release. Inside the B-52 the crew's radio headsets would have been loud with SAM warnings and the frantic beeping of emergency locator beacons triggered by the parachutes of crews that had been shot down. It was a point of honor not to take evasive action during the bomb run.

smart move was to compress the stream, putting more bombers over the target areas in less time. That required precision flying, but the crews were up to it. Solutions were developed for other problems, such as maintenance buildups and the ECM

equipment failures. Also, the intelligence analysts
were put to work to find SAM storage depots, on the
sensible proposition that it was better to bomb them
en masse than encounter them in the air. Several
storage sites were located and added to the target

Uncle Sam goes to war

CHANGING TACTICS:

Map 1 shows the B-52s' flight paths on the first night, when all but six aircraft lumbered down the same route in stately procession. Losses were heavy until new procedures were adopted, like those apparent in map 2. The more complex routes had to be flown with perfect timing, but the highly trained crews had no problems achieving that.

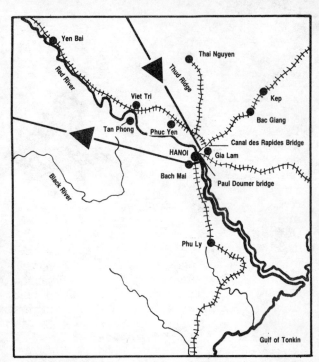

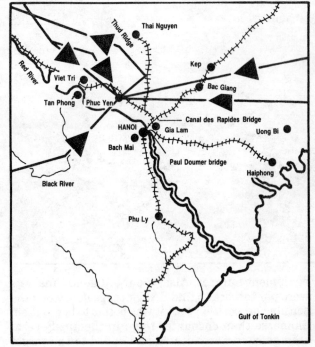

list for 26 December. The strikes on Day Five, 22 December, were all flown by D models from U-Tapao against targets in the Haiphong area. Thirty aircraft were committed. Both approach and exit routes were over the water. As the cells approached Haiphong, they fanned out onto three tracks, then six, confusing the defense system. The Navy suppressed the SAMs so well that only 43 were launched. No aircraft were lost or even damaged, and Haiphong's rail system and petroleum storage areas were blasted. In all, 65 Navy and Air Force aircraft flew support for the 30 bombers: ECM support, chaff drop, chaff escort, MiG CAP, B-52 escort, SAM suppression, and hunter/killer sweeps.

On Day Six, 12 D models from Andersen AFB joined with 18 Ds from U-Tapao to hit SAM sites north of Haiphong, not far from the buffer zone along the Chinese border. Again, the bombers approached and departed over the water. Also, they varied their altitudes and turns in the target area. No bombers were lost.

Bombs away —A USAF Phantom F-4 releases ten MK-36 bombs during an attack over North Vietnam.

No Andersen B-52s were committed against North Vietnam on Day Seven, Christmas Eve. The U-Tapao force flew the usual 30 sorties, supported by 69 support aircraft, blasting rail yards at Kep and Thai Nguyen. The new tactics seemed to work; no aircraft were lost, and only one damaged. On this mission another tail gunner killed a MiG. Airman First Class Albert Moore, a gunner of the 307th Strategic Wing, got the MiG with .50-caliber gunfire.

The entire force paused 36 hours over Christmas Day and into the 26th. If President Nixon expected any gesture from Hanoi during the pause, it did not come. During the pause, the planners and maintenance force made ready for the strikes on the night of 26 December.

Washington had ordered a "maximum effort" against Hanoi for the day after Christmas, and that is what it would get. Seven waves of 120 B-52s were planned, striking ten targets. All seven waves had the same initial time on target, 2230 hours. All bombs would be dropped within the next 15 minutes. Four waves would approach Hanoi from four different directions at the same time. Another wave would strike the Thai Nguyen rail yards north of Hanoi. Two waves were to approach Haiphong from different directions to blast the rail yards and

Uncle Sam goes to war

THE RESULTS: Hanoi power plant before (left) and after (right) a Linebacker raid. B-52s flew 729 sorties and support aircraft flew more than 1,000 in the eleven days of Linebacker II. Losses were 15 B-52s and 11 tactical aircraft. Eight MiG interceptors were shot down. The B-52s dropped more than 49,000 bombs, destroying 1,600 military structures and 373 pieces of railroad rolling stock. Civilian casualties were estimated at between 1,300 to 1,600. The North Vietnamese used up over 1,000 SA-2 missiles.

transformer station. The object was to overload and confuse the defensive system. Support aircraft from Navy, Marine, and Air Force units totaled 113.

All the support would be needed, and all of the new tactics as well. Hanoi's defensive system had enjoyed five days to regroup and restock. They had plenty of SAMs and ammunition for the AAA guns.

Colonel James R. McCarthy was the airborne commander, flying in Wave I. He counted 26 SAMs fired

at his cell, then quit counting. He said, "At bombs away, it looked like we were right in the middle of a fireworks factory that was in the process of blowing up. The radio was completely saturated with SAM calls and MiG warnings."

Two B-52s were hit. One blew up over Hanoi, but four of the crew ejected to become POWs. The pilot of the other one, Captain Jim Turner, flew the damaged B-52D back to U-Tapao, but crashed on the

SAM store —Missile containers in a support area near Thanh Hoa early in 1972. The decision to attack missile stores before the missiles could be deployed and launched saved many lives.

landing attempt. Only two of the six crew members survived. The new tactics of 26 December worked, although two aircraft were lost. Debriefing and analysis of the losses revealed that both aircraft were in two-ship cells, the third ship in both cases having dropped out. The loss of one B-52 from a cell meant that mutual ECM support was weak, and the remaining two aircraft more vulnerable. The solution was to have the remaining two aircraft in such a case join up with the three-ship cell in front or behind.

On the next night, the 27th, the strike force hit Hanoi again with 60 bombers, half from each base. The targets in Haiphong had been knocked out. Against Hanoi, the force would fly in six waves against seven targets, dropping all of the bombs in ten minutes, beginning at 2259 hours. The defenders launched more SAMs than the night before, bagging two B-52s. One, a B-52D from U-Tapao, was flown by Captain John Mize. Its target was a SAM site designated VN-243.

Captain Mize recalled the action, just after his crew had dropped its bombs on VN-243: "I saw 15 SAMs airborne at one time; five to the left, five in front, and five to our right. We successfully evaded 14 of them, but the 15th got us." Mize was wounded in the left thigh, lower leg, and left hand on the control column. The other five crew members were also wounded. All four engines on the left side of the aircraft were shot out, and most of the electrical system was damaged. Incredibly, with all the power on only one side and badly wounded himself, Mize kept the bomber aloft for 48 minutes until across the Laotian border. There he ordered the crew to bail out. They all made it, and were rescued.

The targets for the 28th—the tenth night of bombing—were three SAM sites and a support facility near Hanoi and the key rail yard at Lang Dang. The area of the Lang Dang yards, 60 miles northeast of the capital, was a choke point on both the road and railway from China. Sixty aircraft were assigned, half from U-Tapao and half from Andersen. Again the routes into and out of the targets were varied, as were post-target maneuvers. Time over the target was 2215 hours.

The raids went as planned. Heavy chaff laying, electronic jamming, and SAM suppression by the 99 support aircraft contributed to success. No B-52s were hit or damaged. Returning crews reported erratic SAMs, lighter flak, and saw no MiGs. It appeared that Hanoi might be running out of ammunition.

The eleventh and final night of Linebacker II raids was 29 December. Post-strike analysis of targets hit in earlier days showed that all the valid military targets in the Hanoi and Haiphong areas had suffered enough damage. Only three targets were selected for the last night: two SAM storage areas, where missiles still remained, and the Lang Dang rail yard once more.

Before the briefings, the campaign still looked indefinite. However, the word was floating via the rumor mill that this might be the last day. That was confirmed officially later in the day; bombing north of the 20th Parallel would cease after the mission of the 29th. Colonel Jim McCarthy gave the final briefing. "As the crews filed into the briefing room, I could sense their rising level of confidence. We were closing in for the finale, and they knew it," he said.

Again, 60 B-52s were launched, 30 from each base. Offices all over Andersen AFB closed so their people could see the final launch. When the 30 aircraft from Andersen began taxiing for takeoff, the crews could see at least 8,000 spectators along the flight line and on buildings.

One aircraft from Andersen had to turn back because its refueling system was not working properly. So 59 B-52s made the last strikes of Linebacker II, aided by 102 support aircraft. The first bombs began falling on the targets at 2320 hours. The last bombs fell 23 minutes later, at 2343 hours. Only a few SAMs were fired, and they were erratic. A single MiG showed up but did not press its attack. No aircraft were hit.

When the last B-52G landed at Andersen AFB on the morning of 30 December, that was the end of Linebacker II.

Was it worth the effort?

Dr. Kissinger told a news conference on 24 January: "There was a deadlock...in the middle of December, and there was a rapid movement when negotiations resumed on .. January 3 .. these facts have to be analyzed by each person for himself."

Fast-mover —An RF-101 Voodoo reconnaissance plane above Kep MiG base, northeast of Hanoi, photographed by its wingman flying above. The Voodoo was capable of more than 1,000 mph. Recon crews had the motto "Alone, unarmed, and unafraid," although some argued that "Alone, unarmed, and scared shitless" was closer to the truth.

The final mission

The POWs come home

ON 30 DECEMBER 1972, President Nixon announced in Washington that peace talks would resume in Paris on 8 January. The bombing pause north of the 20th Parallel continued. However, for 15 days Navy, Marine, and Air Force tactical aircraft flew 20 sorties daily against targets south of the 20th Parallel. B-52s added 36 more sorties each day.

The United States announced on 15 January that all offensive action against North Vietnam would stop immediately. The skies over all of North Vietnam were free of strike aircraft.

A week later, on 23 January, Dr. Kissinger and Le Duc Tho signed a cease-fire agreement. The cease-fire went into effect on 27 January 1973. The last B-52 Arc Light strikes on targets in South Vietnam were flown on that day. The last US tactical air strike in South Vietnam was also flown on the 27th by Commander Dennis Weichman. Weichman was the commander of Navy attack squadron VA-153, equipped with A-7E Corsair II aircraft. When he landed aboard the USS *Oriskany* Dennis Weichman completed his 625th combat mission.

Under the cease-fire terms, US prisoners of war began to be released. The first POW returnees left Hanoi's Gia Lam airfield on 12 February. Others were freed in groups over the succeeding weeks. By 29 March, the last of 591 POWs came out, including three held in China, nine in Laos, and one in the hands of the Viet Cong.

The B-52s and strike aircraft continued operating over Cambodia until mid-August. On 15 August, the last Arc Light bombs were dropped on Cambodia.

Later on that same day, Captain Lonnie O. Ratley flew an A-7D Corsair II on a strike mission over

The final mission

THE END: April 1975. This intelligence photo shows vehicles and equipment abandoned by South Vietnamese forces at a river landing point near Hue, just three weeks before the final collapse of South Vietnam. By then forbidden to fly strikes, US airmen were reduced to evacuating refugees to the waiting naval forces, and taking recon pictures to document the final days of South Vietnam.

PHOTO DATE: 8 APRIL 1975

ABANDC
APP

Cambodia. After the strike he flew northwest back to base in Thailand. When his tires streaked onto the runway at Korat, his mission was at an end and with it came the end of American air strikes in Southeast Asia.

Were all the air strikes worth the cost? One person's or one country's assessment is sure to be denied by another. One thing can be said with

AMMUNITION

LST R

certainty, however, about the men who flew strike aircraft during the war in Southeast Asia. They flew the missions assigned them, and carried out their country's orders with skill and bravery.

That the missions had to be flown under rules and controls manipulated by politicians, and against the toughest enemy defenses then existing, does not detract from their performance.

155

AAM	— Air-to-air missile.
AGL	— Height above ground level.
AGM	— Air-to-ground missile.
AGM-45	— Shrike air-to-ground missile.
AGM-78	— Standard arm air-to-ground missile, anti-radiation.
AIM	— Air-intercept missile.
AIM-7	— Sparrow air-to-air missile, semiactive radar type.
AIM-9	— Sidewinder air-to-air missile, passive infrared type.
ALO	— Air liaison officer.
ARC LIGHT	— B-52 operations in Southeast Asia.
ARVN	— Army of South Vietnam.
Bogey	— Term for unidentified aircraft.
BUFF	— Big Ugly Fat Fella—nickname for B-52 bomber.
CBU	— Cluster bomb unit.
CINCPAC	— Commander in chief Pacific.
CTZ	— Corps Tactical Zone.
DASC	— Direct air support center.
DMZ	— Demilitarized Zone.
DRV	— Democratic Republic of Vietnam (North Vietnam).
ECM	— Electronic counter measures.
EOGB	— Electro-Optical guided bomb; smart bomb.
EWO	— Electronic weapons officer.
FAC	— Forward air controller.
Fansong	— Soviet guidance radar.
JCS	— Joint Chiefs of Staff.
LGB	— Laser-guided bomb; smart bomb.
LOC	— Lines of communication.
LZ	— Landing zone.
M-61	— Vulcan cannon.
MAC	— Military airlift command.
MACV	— Military Assistance Command Vietnam.
MAG	— Marine air group.
MiGCAP	— Combat air patrol for MiGs.
Night Owl	— Night strike missions.
NVA	— North Vietnamese Army.
PACAF	— Pacific air forces.

Phantom	— Nickname for F-4 aircraft.
POL	— Petroleum, oil, lubricants.
POW	— Prisoner of war.
RESCAP	— Combat air patrol (for rescue operations).
Route package	— One of seven geographical divisions of North Vietnam.
RVNAF	— Republic of Vietnam Armed Forces.
SA-2	— Soviet-built surface-to-air missile system.
SAC	— Strategic Air Command.
SAM	— Surface-to-air missile.
SAR	— Search and rescue.
Shrike	— Nickname for AGM-45 air-to-ground radar-seeking missile.
Skyhawk	— Nickname for Navy/Marine Corps A-4 attack aircraft.
Shadow	— Nickname for AC-119G gunship.
Sidewinder	— Nickname for AIM-9 infrared missile.
Sparrow	— Nickname for AIM-7 radar-guided missile.
Spectre	— Nickname for AC-130 gunship (Gunship II).
Spooky	— Nickname for AC-47 gunship.
Stinger	— Nickname for AC-119K gunship.
Strike	— An attack upon a surface target.
TAC	— Tactical air command.
TDY	— Temporary duty away from home station.
TFS	— Tactical fighter squadron.
TFW	— Tactical fighter wing.
Thud	— Nickname for the Republic F-105 Thunderchief.
TOT	— Time over target.
TRW	— Tactical reconnaissance wing.
VNAF	— Vietnamese Air Force (South).
Walleye	— Nickname for the AGM-62 air-to-ground missile.
Wild Weasel	— F-100F or F-105F aircraft with radar homing system.
WSO	— Weapon systems officer or whizzo; backseater in the F-4.

About the Author

F. Clifton Berry, Jr.

F. Clifton Berry, Jr., was a paratrooper and airborne infantry officer in the 82d Airborne Division. He saw Vietnam combat as operations officer of the 196th Light Infantry Brigade, logging 600 flying hours in helicopters and FAC aircraft.

In an Army career, he commanded airborne and infantry units from squad through battalion level in the US and Far East.

Following active service, since 1975 he has been an editor and writer on military and aerospace topics. He was co-editor of *Armed Forces Journal*, editor in chief of *AIR FORCE Magazine*, and chief US editor of the Interavia publishing group. He is the author of *Sky Soldiers*, a volume in the Illustrated History of the Vietnam War series.

He is a master parachutist and active pilot, with land and seaplane ratings.

The Illustrated History of
MARINES
The Vietnam War

EDWIN

The Illustrated History of
ARMOR
The Vietnam War

The Illustrated History of
KHE SANH
The Vietnam War

The Illustrated History of
SKY
SOLDIERS
The Vietnam War

E. CLIFTON BERRY, JR

The Illustrated History of
CARRIER
OPERATIONS
The Vietnam War

MICHAEL

EDWARD J. MAROLDA

THE ILLUSTRATED HISTORY OF THE VIETNAM WAR

[...]am's Illustrated History of the [...]am War is a unique and new [...]s of books exploring in depth the [...]hat seared America to the core: [...] that cost 58,022 American lives, [...] saw great heroism and re-[...]efulness mixed with terrible [...]uction and tragedy.

[...] Illustrated History of the Viet-[...]War examines exactly what hap-[...]d: every significant aspect—the [...]cal details, the operations and the strategies behind them—is analyz-ed in short, crisply written original books by established historians and journalists.

Some books are devoted to key bat-tles and campaigns, others unfold the stories of elite groups and fighting units, while others focus on the role of specific weapons and tactics.

Each volume is totally original and is richly illustrated with photographs, line drawings, and maps.